Limited Edition.

Signed by Martin Hellis
on 30th April, 2013.

(Played John in November, 1961
production "The Gateway", Edinburgh.)

D1348282

THE MAN
FROM THERMOPYLAE

by

ADA F. KAY
(A.J. Stewart)

First published 1981
by the Scottish Society of Playwrights

Printed by Peterson Printers 12 Laygate, South Shields Tel: (0632) 563493

Copywright © Scottish Society of Playwrights 346 Sauchiehall Street, Glasgow
ISBN 0 906799 02 3

FOREWORD

My long lasting love affair with A.J. Stewart's, THE MAN FROM THERMOPYLAE, began in Edinburgh during the 1961 Festival. That splendid actress, Lennox Milne, introduced me to the then unpublished manuscript. I read and reread it three times in a single afternoon and was so emotionally stirred by its power and beauty that I impulsively booked a flight the next day for London and a hastily arranged meeting with A.J.

After a marathon luncheon in a West End pub, which sparked a warm, still existing friendship, A.J. agreed to terms that gave me a one year option to secure a first class production of THERMOPYLAE in the United States.

I returned to my California home that fall and started preliminary planning for that long, tedious, frustrating process that inevitably accompanies the financing and production of a play. Before anything meaningful was accomplished, however, I received word from A.J. announcing a late November production of her play at the Gateway Theatre in Edinburgh. After convincing my quite pregnant wife that I had to attend the play's premiere, I made the six thousand mile journey and arrived just in time for the opening.

It was a most rewarding evening. Despite the inevitable flaws that surface at the first performance of any play, the audience reaction was highly favourable.

For the next two weeks I spent all-day, creatively exciting sessions with A.J. in her flat in Leamington Terrace, sessions that yielded a revised script that I was confident would totally captivate American audiences.

Now we deal with harsh reality. That projected American audience never had the opportunity to be captivated. I won't dwell long on the frustrating year that followed. Financial investors, potential co-producers all agreed on the play's dramatic power and beauty, but each in turn sang the same, sad song — too large a cast, too many expensive sets, too little chance for commercial success.

At the end of that disheartening year, I reluctantly relinquished my option on the play, but my enthusiasm and belief in its theatrical future has never abated. So, you can imagine my delight when I was informed that THERMOPYLAE had been chosen for publication by the Scottish Society of Playwrights. How flattered I felt when A.J. requested this foreword.

THERMOPYLAE, like other classic theatre pieces, seems to have taken on a life of its own. Who knows, perhaps some one reading this edition will fall under its spell as I did and take up the quest that I so reluctantly relinquished years ago.

Long live A.J. . . . . . Long live THERMOPYLAE!

Jerry Devine
Los Angeles
27 August 1980

As Ada F. Kay, the author of 'The Man from Thermopylae' and other plays.

As A.J. Stewart, the author of 'Falcon: the autobiography of His Grace James IV, King of Scots' and 'Died 1513, Born 1929: the autobiography of A.J. Stewart'.

SYNOPSIS OF SCENES

Act One

Scene 1   Exterior of a wayside inn on the road from Thermopylae. Morning.

Scene 2   The house of Iolaus, in Sparta. Morning, three weeks later.

Scene 3   Scene as before. One hour later.

Act Two

Scene 1   A chamber in the City Hall. One hour later.

Scene 2   A quiet corner of the city. Half an hour later.

Scene 3   A chamber in the City Hall. Some minutes later.

Act Three

Scene 1   Scene as before. Two minutes later.

Scene 2   A place at the meeting of four roads. Early morning, some months later.

Scene 3   A desolate place upon the cliffs above Thermopylae. Late evening, some weeks later.

CHARACTERS:

GERON

THE GIRL

THE OLD WOMAN

PANTITES

PHILANDER

POLIXENES

MELISSA — Mother of Pantites

PENTHESSILEA — Sister of Pantites

IOLAUS — Father to Pantites

SCORPIAS

HELENA — Wife to Pantites

HIPPIAS — Uncle to Pantites

CLEON

CLEISTHENES

A PRIEST

Servants, voices, etc.

The Man from Thermopylae received its stage premiere at Rheydt, West Germany as Der Mann von den Thermopylen on 11 March 1959 with the following cast:

Pantites, Krieger des Leonidas . . . . .MANFRED LUCHT
Iolaus, Burger von Sparta . . . . HEINZ LORSCHEIDT
Hippias, dessen Bruder . . . . .HANS RUHRDANZ
Melissa, Gattin des Iolaus . . . . .ELISA TUERSCHMANN
Penthesilea, deren Tochter . . . . .SIBYLLE SCHNEIDER
Helena, Gattin des Pantites . . . . .MAJA SCHOLZ
Frixos, Freund des Hauses. . . . . .PERCY ADION
Geron, Landstreicher . . . . HANS GOGUEL A' G.
Orlea, eine Dame in Trauer .GERDA KORDEN
Koryander, Kaufmann . . . . .KARL FRANKEN
Philander, Theaterleiter . . . . .ERNST VOGEL
Diotima. . . . . .SUSANNE SCHONWIESE
Die Gastwirtin . . . . MARGRIT EYCKOFF
Der Mann. . . . . PETER PRANGENBERG
Der Torhuter . . . . .ERNST-ALBERT LUCKER
Der Junge . . . . .HEINZ-HERMANN BERNSTEIN
Hermes . . . . .HANS JOACHIM POST

Director: Knut Roenneke   Sets and Costumes: Roswitha Bormann-Schubert

A FEW SUBSEQUENT PRODUCTIONS

The Edinburgh Gateway Company opened their production of The Man from Thermopylae at the Gateway Theatre, Edinburgh on 14 November 1961 with the following cast:

Geron . . . . .TOM FLEMING
Girl. . . . . MARJORIE HENDERSON
Innkeeper . . . . JEAN TAYLOR SMITH
Pantites. . . . . VICTOR CARIN
Melissa, his mother . . . . MARILYN GRAY
Iolaus, his father . . . . .MARTIN HELLER
Hippias, his uncle . . . . WALLACE CAMPBELL
Helena, his wife. . . . . .MARGO CROAN
Orlea. . . . . CHRISTINA GRAY
Servants. . . . . DAVID STRONG, JOHN DUNCANSON
Penthessilea, sister to Pantites . . . . ROSEMARY EADIE
Cleon   . . . . .BROWN DERBY
Scorpias   Spartan Elders . . . . .PAUL KERMACK
Clisthenes   . . . . .JAMES GIBSON
Priest . . . . .DAVID STRONG
Philander. . . . . .BRYDEN MURDOCH
Polixenes. . . . . .JOHN DUNCANSON
Twins . . . . .MARGO CROAN, MARJORIE HENDERSON
Bearded Lady. . . . . .CHRISTINA GRAY

Director: Tom Fleming   Sets and Costumes: David Lovett

The Arts Theatre Company opened their production under the title March Home Tomorrow at the Ipswich Arts Theatre on 17 November 1964 with the following cast:

Geron . . . . JOHN RUTLAND
The Girl. . . . . CLAIRE LUCKHAM
The Old Woman . . . . HANNAH GORDON
Philander . . . . KENNETH POITEVIN
Polixenes . . . . LAURIE ASPREY
Pantites . . . . GARY BOND
Melissa — mother to Pantites . . . . JANET HENFREY
Penthessilea — sister to Pantites . . . . .PAULINE MASON
Cleon . . . . BRIAN HAWKESLEY
Scorpias. . . . . ALAN PARTINGTON
Hippias — uncle to Pantites . . . . .ALAN JUDD
Helena — wife to Pantites . . . . HANNAH GORDON
Clisthenes . . . . .RAYMOND BOWERS
A Priest . . . . ANDREW McWHIRTER
Servants and Crowd

Producer: Robert Chetwyn   Sets and Costumes: Geoffrey Scott

The Edinburgh Gateway Company presented The Man From Thermopylae as part of the Edinburgh International Festival at the Gateway Theatre, Edinburgh. The opening performance was on 23 August 1965 and had the following cast:

Geron . . . . BERNARD LLOYD
Girl. . . . . .ROSEMARY CURR
Old Woman . . . . JEAN TAYLOR SMITH
Pantites . . . . VICTOR CARIN
Philander . . . . .BRYDEN MURDOCH
Polixenes . . . . TONY KINNIE
Melissa, mother of Pantites . . . . .CLARE RICHARDS
Penthessilea, sister of Pantites . . . . .JUDITY CAREY
Iolaus, father of Pantites. .WILLIAM MOORE
Scorpias. . . . . .BRIAN CAREY
Helena, wife of Pantites . . . . JENNIFER CLAIRE
Hippias, uncle of Pantites . . . . .JAMES LOCKER
Cleon . . . . BROWN DERBY
Cleisthenes. . . . . JAMES GIBSON
Priest . . . . .TED RICHARDS
Servants, Voices . . . . . MICHAEL SUGDEN, SIMON BETTS, ALISON KEY,
                          TONY KINNIE, ROSEMARY CURR, TED RICHARDS

Director: Richard Mathews   Designer: Hamish Henderson

Joe Pasternak, Harlequin presented the American premiere of The Man From Thermopylae at the Masquers Theatre in Hollywood on 24 October 1972 with the following cast:

The Girl. . . . . .SHIRLEY WALKER
Innkeeper . . . . KATHLEEN O'MALLEY
Geron . . . . .SEAN McCLORY
Pantites . . . . .ARON KINCAID
Philander . . . . STANLEY ADAMS
Polyxenes . . . . .ANGELO ROSSITTO
Penthessilea . . . . .MARINA BENJAMIN
Melissa . . . . .ALICE DUDLEY
Iolaus . . . . PHILIP CARY JONES
Helena. . . . . .JOICY REVIS
Hippias . . . . FRANCIS De SALES
Clisthenes . . . . .JONATHAN HOLE
Scorpias. . . . . LLOYD PETER OLIPHANT
Cleon . . . . MAURICE MANSON
Priest . . . . .KEVIN G. TRACEY
Hermes . . . . RICK GATES
Servants. . . . . . IRENE McNAMARA, MARK ROEMER, GEORGE SPELVIN

Directed and Designed by: Kay E. Kuter

ACT ONE

SCENE 1

The exterior of an Inn on the road from Thermopylae.

There are benches outside the Inn, and a rough table bearing empty cups and an earthenware pitcher — also a basket containing a baby.

Upon a bench, dozing in the sun, sits Geron, an ancient, ragged figure. Down R. stands a girl, motionless, her empty eyes fixed upon the road toward Thermopylae. The birds sing, the sky is clear, and the baby cries loudly from the basket. It is morning.

The old woman shouts from the dark interior of the Inn.

OLD WOMAN   Dear mercy on us! *She appears angrily in the doorway.* Girl, I have warned you — if you cannot quieten that brat of yours, I shall turn both of you out on to the road to beg for your bread. *The girl shows no awareness.* There is water to be drawn, and the fire dies for lack of wood . . . *The girl pays no heed. The baby whimpers into silence. The old woman goes to the girl and shakes her shoulder in exasperation.* Girl! Bestir yourself. Girl! *It is no use. The old woman turns to Geron.* She has been taken this way ever since the first news of the battle. All day she stands there with her eyes on the road, lost in that mad slow dream. *She shouts once more.* Girl! Girl!

GERON   Perhaps if you called her by name . . .?

OLD WOMAN   Name? A beggar's bastard and a soldiers' whore — she has no name. And none to give that brat of hers. She says he was fathered by Achelon, the Thespian . . . ay, well, the claim is safe enough, for none will come back now to deny it. *She turns to go back into the Inn.*

GERON   You will allow the girl no hope?

OLD WOMAN	Hope? Now what use to her is hope? We have had both Greek and Persian pass this way, and all report the same — there were no survivors.
GERON	It is but two days since the battle ended —
OLD WOMAN	Ay — two days! And a man walking from Thermopylae would have been here within the hour. *Over her shoulder to the girl,* I tell you, girl, you can forget that soldier friend of yours. Alive or dead, you can rely on it he has forgotten you. When there is a brat to show for their misdeeds they are all the same, gone like yesterday.
GERON	You speak with authority?
OLD WOMAN	I was a soldiers' whore myself. *As she passes the table, she bangs the pitcher angrily.* Girl! I need water from the well. *No result. Exasperated, she turns back into the Inn — rounding on Geron from the doorway.* And you, too, had best be up and gone. It is a Inn I keep, not a beggar's lodging house. *Geron gives her a mild glance which in some way disconcerts her. She is reduced to a defensive grumble as she goes.* It is bad for the trade, having a beggar on the step . . .

> *The baby begins to howl.*
>
> *Geron glances at the girl, but she pays no attention. He rises and goes to the basket himself, speaking to the baby.*

GERON	Your discourse, sir, has resonance if not vocabulary.

> *The howls rise indignantly.*

Geron listens — then nods in sympathy. Your protest is well justified. Life, sir, is a villainous affliction every one of us were better born without — and the only revenge allowed us is the facility for wishing it on someone else.

> *The child's cries cease, recognising sympathy.*
>
> *From within the Inn comes the sound of a dog barking — then a yelp.*

16

OLD WOMAN	*Off.* Lie down you brute!
GERON	*Looking out front, up the road towards Thermopylae.* Now who is this, alone upon the road . . .? Is it he for whom your mother waits . . .? Or — could it be . . .? *He shows increasing interest as Pantites approaches — turning the basket so that its occupant can see who comes.* Child . . . child — look well upon his face, for this man wears honesty like a garland . . .
	Pantites enters from front and mounts the stage. He surveys everything around him with quiet pleasure. He is tossing a pebble in his hand — not mechanically, but with conscious delight, as if the game were newly discovered that morning.
	Pantites wears a rag of what was once a Spartan soldier's uniform, and on his thigh can be seen the dried blood of a wound. He walks with a limp, but through his weariness shines the wondering, ingenuous joy of one to whom life itself is still a novelty.
PANTITES	Good day to you, sir!
GERON	Friend, you may have the pleasure of it. Is this child yours?
PANTITES	That is a very personal question, sir, upon so brief acquaintance.
GERON	Then you are not he.
PANTITES	No. I am not he. *He sets himself stiffly on the bench and sighs with relief. He stretches out his leg to examine his wound.*
GERON	You have come from Thermopylae?
PANTITES	I was there — once. *He leans back wearily, closing his eyes against the sunlight.*

17

GERON	*Eagerly.* Then you were a witness to the battle? Report has it that the Spartans are all dead, King Leonidas and his three hundred.
PANTITES	*After a pause, flatly.* Two hundred and ninety-nine. *Geron looks at him. A pause, then* -- Oh, it was purely accidental, I assure you.
GERON	I see . . . how did it happen?
PANTITES	That I only wish I could remember!
GERON	Think back . . .
PANTITES	To what?
GERON	Before the battle. There must have been a plan?
PANTITES	*Frowning, he digs the fragments from his memory.* Our massed armies were to await the Persians on the shore, and there to destroy them. Then . . . our scouts reported that a force had penetrated inland — meaning to descend the cliff and take us in the rear . . . The Greek Commanders decided to withdraw while there was time — except Leonidas. The Thespians, they, too, were to stay — but I know not what became of them. Our orders were plain enough, we were to take up positions along the line of the old Phocian Wall, and there remain.
GERON	Facing an army of six thousand?
PANTITES	Oh, we were not expected to win, the order was to stay.
GERON	I see . . .
PANTITES	*Quite matter of fact, he chuckles a little at the memory.* We took the Persians off their guard, though — rushing into the attack before they even knew the battle had started! Xerxes must have been furious! The gods alone knew what their losses must have been. But Leonidas was killed in that assault — others, too; out of three hundred more than we could spare. The Persian line had reformed then, with reinforcement, and we had to abandon the Wall. Those of us that were left drew together on a hillock to make one final stand. The

Persians poured upon us in waves, like the sea — God, I
have never seen so many men! Hand to hand we met
them, but as fast as one was slain, there sprang up forty
to take his place. *He frowns, finding it now more
difficult to remember.* Our circle was broken. They were
upon all sides and in the midst of us. At most, I think
there cannot have been more than seven of us left . . .
And there my memory ends. *He touches the back of his
head gingerly.* I would say, from the feel of it, that the
blow came from behind. My helmet lies there yet, cleft
like a nutshell.

GERON   And then . . . ?

PANTITES   There is . . . a redness before the eyes, when the sun
beats down on their shuttering lids — that I remember.
And a tickling pain in my thigh . . . Most of all — the
silence; it lay on my ears like a winding sheet. I opened
my eyes. What I expected is hard to say — the Fields of
Elysium, perhaps, and my comrades scratching themselves in the sun . . . Instead, there was a dead, torn eye
staring into my own, and what remained of a face,
rippling black with flies . . . I tell you, I was on my feet
before I gave another thought to anything! *He pauses,
remembering clearly now.* There were the cliffs — and
there, the sea — and there, the Phocian Wall . . . but
where had been noise and men was silence, and everywhere the dead; every slope covered, every hollow
brimming with the dead. Even the sea was hushed and
the waves seemed to lie without movement where they
touched the shore. I have never known such loneliness
as then. In panic, I picked up my sword, meaning to
despatch myself at once after my comrades. And then —
a wave, caught by the sun, broke, like a peal of bells
along the sand; above me a lark burst suddenly into
song — and, in a moment, death became infinitely
undesirable . . . ! *He is almost laughing in the remembered
joy of it.*

GERON   *Could not be gloomier.* Oh dear, dear, dear . . . ! I think,
young man, the gods owe you an apology.

PANTITES   *Astonished.* For sparing my life?

GERON   It is a lamentable oversight.

PANTITES   *Stretching his arms with sensuous enjoyment.* Then

19

Apollo shall have my thanks for it!

Geron watches him, unsmiling.

*The baby breaks suddenly into loud howls.
Pantites goes to the basket. He adjusts the
infant's wrappings, and chucks it under the
chin. The child chuckles.*

GERON   Are you a father?

PANTITES   Not to my knowledge. *He moves away from the basket.*
                 But I have a young sister, born when I was ten years
                 old. I well remember that day, I have never in my life
                 had such a flogging. *He laughs.* I played truant from the
                 Academy, to go home and see her. I got a thrashing from
                 my father, who sent me back at once; another from my
                 uncle, who treated it as mutiny; and a third from my
                 tutor, who in addition made me write out five thousand
                 times "I have no mother but Sparta"!

GERON   And after that, were you convinced?

PANTITES   Eventually. Oh, I know it is said in other states that our
                 way of life is harsh, and so it may be; where else,
                 though, but in Sparta, do you find soldiers of the calibre
                 that stand three hundred to the field and die to order?

GERON   *After the merest pause.* Two hundred and ninety-nine.

PANTITES   *Annoyed.* I have told you, that was an accident! It is not
                 Spartan training at fault because some Persian soldier
                 struck not deep enough.

GERON   True; but does not your soldier's manual give you
                 instructions what to do in such predicament?

PANTITES   *Frowning.* The field manual cannot foresee everything —

GERON   Then, after this, they will doubtless amend the text, and
                 you will enjoy a moderate fame for establishing a
                 precedent. *He speaks with gentle irony.*

PANTITES   *However, takes this seriously, he is quite cheerful about
                 it.* I wonder if I shall? My survival is certain to be the
                 subject of a formal enquiry — there is one held after
                 every battle. It should be interesting.

20

GERON	It should.
PANTITES	Had it been a case of voluntary survival, the question of cowardice would arise; I am glad to be safe from that. It is a good thing I did not lose my sword — even accidentally I found it near my hand when I awoke — it has my number on it, so I know it is my own. *He draws his sword half from the scabbard to look at it affectionately, and pats the scabbard as he slips it back.*
GERON	Do you think you will use it again?
PANTITES	*Amused.* Of course I shall use it again! I am a soldier.
GERON	Oh no, my friend. You were a soldier. This morning when you chose to remain alive —
PANTITES	*Staring at him.* But what use would it have been to anyone had I done otherwise? Had I died in battle two days ago — yes; that made sense. But this morning —
GERON	— This morning, you stepped outside the book of rules, and the pages slammed together like a door behind you.
PANTITES	*Staring at him, half amused, half uneasy.* You speak, sir, like the Delphic Oracle!
GERON	*Sourly.* I was the Delphic Oracle. *He rises and moves away.*
	Pantites stares at him, not knowing what to make of this.
	They are interrupted at this point by the arrival of Philander's Circus. Behind the Inn, we catch a glimpse of gay pennants and streamers which fly from the tops of the wagons, and there can be heard the creak and rumble of their wooden wheels and the hoofbeats of horses, the jingle of bridle bells and the sound of voices and laughter.
PHILANDER	*Off. Shouting.* Nay — the rest of you go on. If we call a halt now, we shall lose the best part of the morning.
	Philander appears up C., carrying a collection of

21

*wine skins. He turns to address an unseen
companion.*

Polixenes, stay you with the horses — *He is cut short by
a screech of laughter from the unseen dwarf, and a well-
aimed ball hits him in the midriff. Laughing, Philander
rescues the ball.* None of your tricks — we have no time.
*He tosses back the ball, which brings another screen of
laughter from the dwarf.*

> *Philander crosses the Inn yard, flourishing a
> hand in greeting to Pantites and Geron.
> Polixenes follows him. Polixenes has the vacant
> happy smile of an imbecile, but he is in his own
> way bright enough.*

A rare fine morning, sirs!

PANTITES

Responding instantly to the warmth of the man.
I cannot recall a better.

> *Geron looks gloomily at them both and grunts
> a cheerless greeting.*

> *The old woman appears in the doorway as
> Philander brings his wineskins.*

PHILANDER

Five skins of wine — and let it be the best you have.

OLD WOMAN

Good wine is scarce.

PHILANDER

Ay, and costly, too, now you have to entertain our
friends, the enemy. *He hands her the skins.* And I want
them full.

> *With a surly glance the old woman turns back
> into the Inn.*

> *Philander turns — warned by a screech of glee
> in time to catch the ball. He tosses it back with
> an affectionate but firm admonishment.*

Enough of that, Polixenes!

> *He turns to Geron and Pantites.*

I shall not be sorry to show the neighbourhood my
heels. A week ago you could feed two men for what it
costs today to fill a horse's nosebag.

PANTITES

You travel far?

22

PHILANDER	To Olympia. We should do good business upon the road with the crowds going to the Games. I am a Philander, sir — of Philander's Circus. If you have not heard of us before, it is a certain thing that you will hear of us again, — everybody knows Philander's Circus.
PANTITES	*Suddenly.* Yours were the tents I saw, pitched in a field outwith the walls of Alpenni — !
PHILANDER	Ay — and you are a soldier, sir. Then it is likely we have met before.
PANTITES	I doubt it, friend. I am a Spartan.
PHILANDER	Ah . . . ! I did hear that the circus had been put out-of-bounds to the Spartans. *Turning to Geron.* And you, friend — do you dwell locally?
GERON	I dwell, sir, where there is a rock to make a windbreak, and a fold of the night black sky to tuck about my ears.
PHILANDER	You are a beggar?
GERON	I would more properly describe myself as a professional philanthropist.
PHILANDER	How so?
GERON	To give alms to a beggar is an act of charity, and charity is held to be a major virtue. Agreed? So, for the price of one small coin, I bestow upon murderers, swindlers and hypocrites, one grain of virtue to offset their black account. Is that not philanthropy? *Philander laughs his agreement. Then he notices Pantites dabbing his wound.*
PHILANDER	Friend, that would needs tending. *He calls.* Woman! — bring the Spartan a bowl of water and clean rags.
PANTITES	Sir — I cannot pay!

23

PHILANDER	A condition not unknown to me. Upon the road you have one prosperous day for every two that you go hungry.
	To Geron.
	Is that not a fact? So you are in good company, soldier. *He produces his purse. Geron eyes it.*
GERON	Your circus did good business . . .
PHILANDER	Ay — six weeks we were pitched at Alpenni. Every day unbroken summer, and all the states of Greece spilling their soldiers into the encampment there. And where the soldiers are, the local girls come flocking. To see the crowds that filled our show-booths, you would have thought the world had called a holiday. Then came the battle. Within a moment, soldiers, girls, and summer, all were gone. There is no call for a circus now in Alpenni.
	There is a screech of laughter and Polixenes comes bounding into the company. He tugs at Philander's hand.
	Yes, Polixenes. We must go. But our friends here have not seen the circus — quickly, show them a sample of your tricks.
	Polixenes gives a short demonstration — tumbling, juggling, whatever suits the actor — while the old woman enters with the bowl of water and rags, crossing with them to Pantites. She looks with distaste upon the dwarf.
OLD WOMAN	You have not brought that creature here again?
	She returns indoors for the wineskins, and brings them as Polixenes ends his act.
PHILANDER	Do you think I would buy wine without my Cellarer's verdict on it?
	Both Philander and Polixenes taste the wine. They look at each other. They are not impressed, but they have tasted worse.
OLD WOMAN	*Annoyed.* What would I have to gain by selling sour wine to a regular customer?

PHILANDER	Nothing. Which causes me to wonder why you try the trick so often.
OLD WOMAN	That is my best wine. Only yesterday a Persian troop was here and drank five jars of it.
PANTITES	*Shocked.* Woman, are you not a Greek?
OLD WOMAN	I am an innkeeper, sir, and both sides are thirsty.
PHILANDER	*Handing the skins to Polixenes.* Hang them high within the wagon, Polixenes — this road travels with the sun.

Polixenes exits with the wineskins.

OLD WOMAN	Here, I have not been paid — *Philander pays her, and pays her well — but she scowls at the money.* Am I to be content with this? Five skins of my best wine — !
PHILANDER	For which I have given you three times their worth — and the price in Alpenni is not yet more than doubled.
OLD WOMAN	There was the bowl of water and the rags. Since the battle you would be amazed how the price of bandaging has risen in these parts.
PHILANDER	*Eyeing her sternly, but not unkindly.* You are well paid.

She glowers at him, but departs.

And we must be on our way. A good day to you, sirs — and may Asclepius speed the healing of your wound.

PANTITES	Thank you, sir.
PHILANDER	*To Geron.* Though I have not committed murder yet, nor hypocrisy, I hope, too often — it behoves me to avail myself of your professional services. *He tosses a coin to Geron, and departs with a wave of his hand.*
GERON	Luck attend you to Olympia!
PHILANDER	*Off.* The gods be with you!

There comes the sound of the circus wagon departing.

GERON	Oh, had I but known there was a circus pitched at Alpenni! Those are the nimblest fingers that ever teased a purse string from a belt.
PANTITES	*Curiously.* But did I not hear you say that you had served the Oracle at Delphi?
GERON	You did.
PANTITES	You were a priest — attendant on the prophetess?
GERON	Prophetess? That drug-sodden female lunatic? Young man, mine was the brain that sweated out the answers to those conundrums.
PANTITES	But this is blasphemy! You speak of a Holy Woman — the voice and wisdom of Apollo — !
GERON	Oh dear . . . It is the credulity of people like you which makes charlatans of men like me.
PANTITES	And Apollo allows this deception?
GERON	Why not? His reputation stands to profit by it just as much as ours.
PANTITES	This is monstrous! That the priesthood should deceive us is bad enough, but to find that the gods can be a party to deceit . . . ! Unless . . .
GERON	There are no gods?
PANTITES	*With a quick upward glance.* I did not say that!
GERON	No — but I recognise the thought. When they find a void within the shrine, the laiety always jumps to that conclusion. Do you honestly think it makes any difference to the gods whether we believe in them or not?
PANTITES	It makes a considerable difference to me!
GERON	The egotism of our human race is really quite remarkable! When you plant a seed, do you inform it

	that it was planted by your hand? And in order to bloom in its appointed place, does the seed have to know the lay-out of the garden?
PANTITES	But there is no comparison — !
GERON	No! We cannot conceive of an intellect superior to our own! It is fit that seeds and rocks and children should be spared from knowing all the facts of life, but we cannot accept that there should be mysteries of which man himself could conveniently be left in ignorance! So we build temples to house our gods — and lose faith if they do not at once move in, visibly, with their baggage and their furniture! We delegate priests and prophets to bother heaven for a daily bulletin upon our most minute affairs — as if Zeus would have given us a brain, had he not intended us to use it! You say heaven should have more contact with men? — dear heaven defend itself! No! Let us leave the Gods in peace, poor overworked creatosrs, and do for ourselves the best we can with the equipment they provided. And should we need the swish of a curtain and the clang of a bell to help us convince ourselves, let us not blame Apollo for giving his blessing to the practice and leaving us to get on with it!
PANTITES	You speak with feeling, sir?
GERON	Religion is my trade.
PANTITES	And my trade is soldiering, so I will leave the argument to you.
	He picks up his cloak.
GERON	What is your next move?
PANTITES	I must return to Sparta.
GERON	Return to Sparta ... ?
PANTITES	My city is at war, and the pick of its men are dead. The Army will have plenty of use for me.
GERON	My friend ... there was a day when kings offered their treasury for my advice. I give it now as a beggar's sole

possession. If you do have those at home you love — go back to Thermopylae and die!

PANTITES   *Incredulous, but not amused.* Go back to Thermopylae and die — ?

> *But the old man's words make him uneasy despite himself. He takes a step towards the road from which he came, and stands for a moment looking — like the girl — towards Thermopylae.*

Go back and die . . . Go back and die? — *He has rejected the idea now, with its uneasiness. He is incredulous and amused a little.* With a family and a young wife at home — who waits as that girl waits?

> *He moves back C. — a bird breaks suddenly into song, soaring above him. He throws back his head to watch its flight, smiling in his delight.*

Return to Thermopylae and die — while the world holds one morning such as this? *He throws the cloak over his shoulders.* No! I take the homeward road — to Sparta!

GERON   *Watching him with interest.* Can I ask of you a favour?

PANTITES   What I have is yours.

GERON   Grant me your company upon the road.

PANTITES   The concession, sir, is yours — the privilege, mine.

> *They exchange a bow.*

How do I call you, sir? My name is Pantites.

GERON   Mine, sir, is Geron.

> *He pulls his rags more closely about him and reaches for his staff.*

PANTITES   If I may ask, what takes you to Sparta?

GERON   *As they go off.* Curiosity, sir . . . curiosity . . .

CURTAIN

SCENE 2

The House of Iolaus, in Sparta.

Time: Morning, one month later.

Penthessilea, a girl of about sixteen, sits frowning over her poem. Dissatisfied, she alters words and phrases, murmuring them over to herself. She uses a stylus and a wax tablet which folds like a small wooden notebook. She is completely absorbed in what she is doing. So far as we can hear the lines which give her trouble, they are —

PENTHESSILEA   "Though Sparta mourns, her tears are proud; greater than grief, her pride excels; all history — and (something) — avowed (something) — etc.

Melissa enters quietly R.

MELISSA   Still working on your poem.

PENTHESSILEA   I wish I could get it right! The last verse is so clumsy . . .

MELISSA   No-one will worry about that, if it is written with sincerity.

PENTHESSILEA   Will they not? You should hear the girls at school! Some think Herione would have been asked to write the poem for the Fallen, because she had her brother and her father killed.

A pause.

Has the dressmaker gone?

MELISSA   Yes.

PENTHESSILEA   *Eagerly, putting down the tablet and stylus.* Oh, can I see the dress? You and Helena are lucky to be going to the Palace! While the Queen was inviting mothers and widows of the fallen, I do think she might have invited sisters, too.

MELISSA	*A slight pause. A sigh.* Child, you know not what you are saying. Perhaps tomorrow you will understand, when you have to face the ordeal of public ceremony.
	A pause.
	Would you like me to read your poem?
PENTHESSILEA	Oh, yes, Mother — please. But will you please not read the last verse yet? I shall have to alter that third line. The second line would scan all right if I had —
	In the process of handing over the poem, she is interrupted by a commotion outside, and the hurried entrance of Scorpias C.
SCORPIAS	Iolaus! Iolaus — *Seeing Melissa.* Melissa — your pardon, Madam —
MELISSA	You seek my husband, Scorpias?
SCORPIAS	At once! He is required at the City Hall immediately. *He mops his brow.*
MELISSA	*Handing back the poem to Penthessilea and urging her away.* Penthessilea, go quickly. Call your father.
	Penthessilea hurries out L.
	To Scorpias. Iolaus is in his study. He will be here in a moment.
SCORPIAS	*Pacing resltessly, he spills his tale to Melissa, being unable to keep it to himself.* That such a thing could happen . . . ! Melissa — imagine it! — one of the men who died at Thermopylae has come back!
MELISSA	*A gasp.* What . . . ?
SCORPIAS	*Quite unconscious of the personal implication to Melissa, he hurries on.* One of the men reported dead — he arrived at the North City Gate just half an hour ago.
MELISSA	Scorpias . . . who is the man?
SCORPIAS	I cannot tell you. The message from the Guard Commander made no mention of his name. Imagine it . . . !

He looks out of the window at the memorial. I suppose I shall have to order work to stop on the Memorial — temporarily, at least. Over two hundred names have been inscribed already — two hundred! It is a record achievement, you know, even for the Public Works Department — and if he is one of those already listed dead . . . oh, the work that will need to be done again — the cost in labour and materials — !

> *Iolaus enters, followed by Penthessilea.*

SCORPIAS

Iolaus, Cleon needs you at the City Hall immediately.

MELISSA

Her voice calm after that of Scorpias. One of the men reported dead has returned.

IOLAUS

From Thermopylae . . . ? *He stares at her.*

MELISSA

He has not yet been identified.

SCORPIAS

Cutting through her calm, he is edging Iolaus towards the exit C. Iolaus, we must hurry. Cleon wants your legal opinion before he calls a meeting of the City Elders.

> *Iolaus gives Melissa a long look before he goes out with Scorpias.*

As they go out. In my opinion, the man had no right to make public his survival until he had consulted us. To take lodgings outside the city, and quietly send us word — it was the least he could have done. It would have given us time to arrange a formal welcome. Just to stroll in through the City Gate, it really is not good enough. . .

> *Left alone, Melissa stands for a moment very still, her eyes closed. The shock has exhausted her. During the scene with Scorpias, Penthessilea has been standing up L. In the shadows listening. Now she creeps forward — still clutching her poem, as if unconsciously defending it.*

PENTHESSILEA

Mother . . . what does it mean?

> *Melissa turns and shakes her head, baffled. She straightens the neckline of Penthessilea's dress and puts in place a strand of her hair. Her movements are automatic, and she says nothing.*

If one of the men has come back . . . what will happen?

MELISSA

I have no idea. *She takes Penthessilea by the arm.* Come, let us walk in the garden. You shall read your poem to me. While we wait —

PENTHESSILEA

Wait, mother? Wait for what?

MELISSA

Oh . . . for anything — for nothing — I know not which. But waiting is a woman's traditional occupation, Penthessilea — have you not yet learned that?

They go out L.

The stage is empty for some moments. Then Pantites and Geron appear up C. in the entrance from the street.

PANTITES

Geron — welcome to my father's house.

He motions Geron to enter. Geron limps a little as he crosses the threshold.

GERON

Pantites, you have walked my feet off.

PANTITES

And you have talked my head off, so we are even. *He glances about him.* No-one to receive us? *He goes up to the bell hanging by the door and sets it clanging, then he pauses in thought.* Geron, can it be they have not heard the news?

GERON

Oh, they will have heard the news. By now, everyone in Sparta will have heard the news. You should have taken my advice, and entered the city quietly by night.

PANTITES

I am a Spartan citizen, not a thief! I tell you, you have been about your trade too long, old friend.

GERON

It would have spared you the inquisition at the city gate.

PANTITES

The Guard Commander merely did his duty. No city allows strangers within its walls unchallenged.

GERON

You are not a stranger.

PANTITES	I am a man returned from the dead — an equally dubious condition.
GERON	I can feel now their eyes upon us as we walked away, and the silence in the street that bore us company . . .
PANTITES	I wish you would forget it! I am more concerned about the silence here. Where is everyone?
	He sets the bell clanging a second time. After a moment, Melissa enters L. and pauses, staring at him incredulously — then.
MELISSA	Pantites!
PANTITES	Mother!
	Melissa runs into his arms, sobbing his name joyfully. They embrace.
MELISSA	Pantites! My son — ! It is you! You are alive! I cannot believe it . . . ! Are you wounded? I see no wound — oh yes, that is a new scar on your cheek. Oh — you are alive! — alive! I cannot believe it . . . ! *She hugs him, alternately weeping and laughing with joy. Geron moves tactfully away a little distance.*
PANTITES	Yes, Mother — I am alive. Apollo have my thanks for it!
MELISSA	We heard that there was one returned, but I did not think — I dare not hope — *She weeps afresh.*
PANTITES	Mother, I am alive — it is no cause for weeping!
MELISSA	Forgive me — it is the shock of seeing you. I did not show my tears, though, when you were reported dead. I promise you — except a little privately.
PANTITES	*Remembering Geron.* Oh — Mother, let me introduce my friend, Geron. He came with me upon the road.
MELISSA	*Turning with a welcoming gesture to Geron.* Welcome, sir, to my husband's house.
GERON	*Bowing.* Blessings upon your hearth.
	Penthessilea appears up L. and pauses, very still.

33

PENTHESSILEA	Pantites!
PANTITES	*Joyfully, swinging round.* Penthessilea! *He holds out his arms to her, but she does not run to him. She takes a step forward, then stops, looking from Pantites to her mother.*
PENTHESSILEA	They did not say it was you . . . !
	Puzzled, Pantites slowly lowers his arms. He looks at his mother. There is an awkward silence.
MELISSA	*Quickly.* Penthessilea — we have a guest. Geron — sir — this is my daughter. She will conduct you to your room, and call a servant to attend your needs.
GERON	*Bowing.* Madam.
MELISSA	*A warning note as Penthessilea makes no move.* Penthessilea — !
PENTHESSILEA	*Swallowing a great deal that she would like to say.* Yes, mother. Come, sir.
	She departs R. with another bow to Melissa Geron follows Penthessilea — at a distance, indulgently. Melissa turns to Pantites, anxious to cover the embarrassment.
MELISSA	Pantites, dear —
PANTITES	*Staring amazed after the departed Penthessilea.* What did she mean?
MELISSA	Pay no attention to her, dear. You know how moody young girls are at that age, and so unpredictable in their reactions.
PANTITES	Yes, but . . . I should like to know what she meant.
MELISSA	Oh, it was nothing dear. Her head is full of romantic notions. Since the battle she has barely touched her food, and sits all day in her room writing poetry. To-

	morrow she was to have read one of her poems in the memorial ceremony at school.
PANTITES	Memorial ceremony?
MELISSA	To the Fallen — of Thermopylae. Naturally, I suppose she was looking forward to all the . . . *Her voice tails off as she realises how this must sound. There is an uneasy pause between them.*
PANTITES	I see. Where is my wife?
MELISSA	At the Palace, dear.
PANTITES	What is she doing there?
MELISSA	Well . . . she was invited by Her Majesty to serve on the Committee . . .
PANTITES	*More and more baffled.* Committee?
MELISSA	Yes; the Queen is holding a reception this afternoon — for the widows and mothers of the Fallen. And any function has to be organised by a committee. Naturally.
PANTITES	I see . . .
MELISSA	*Changing the subject.* Now tell me, what happened to you? What miracle has brought you back alive?
PANTITES	I awoke, among the dead. That is all I know.
MELISSA	My thanks to Hera! *She dabs away fresh tears.* These tears again — I am ashamed! Forgive me.
PANTITES	*Suddenly.* Why should you not weep? Why not? It is a sign of human feeling.
MELISSA	*Uneasily.* Pantites . . .
PANTITES	I know. Patriotism is the only respectable emotion recognised within our city.

35

MELISSA	*Swiftly.* Dear, I am forgetting my duties. You have not eaten. Nor have I even offered you a cup of wine —
PANTITES	*Prowling restlessly.* Returning here, I passed through many parts of Greece. Upon the road, I saw and sometimes shared another way of life than ours. I saw lovers walk together — in broad daylight — with their arms entwined. I saw women kiss their children — openly, Mother, in the street! — and not once did their menfolk chide them for it!
MELISSA	*Disturbed.* Those were peasant women —
PANTITES	They were women! I saw it more than once, a lady of our own rank carrying her baby, while the nursemaid walked behind her empty-handed.
MELISSA	*Quite sharply.* Such customs may prevail in other states, but here in Sparta —
PANTITES ·	Here, in Sparta, if you pat your child upon the head it is an act of treason!

A pause.

MELISSA	*Her voice restrained and flat in its recital.* Pantites . . . Your brother was a comely child, and healthy, but there was no way that I could hide his blindness. The Elders spoke kindly, they assured me that he would be better dead. And I believe them. *With a sharp, slight turn.* I know! You will tell me that you saw in other cities blind men at a potter's wheel, as skilled — and happy! — as their fellows who have sight. That I have heard. But blind men do not make good soldiers. And your brother happened to be born in Sparta: as I was born in Sparta.

A pause.

Her voice changes, to the sweet, domestic tone that is normal with her. Dear, I must have the servants prepare a bath for you — and you must rest a while after your journey. There is a tunic which you left behind — I had it pressed and hung for you, should you come back.

PANTITES	*Glances at her sharply.* Should I come back?

Geron enters R.

MELISSA — *Seeing him.* I am neglecting hospitality. A cup of wine to refresh you — I will send for it at once.

She exits quickly R.

GERON — Forgive me. I returned too soon.

PANTITES — Too soon? For her, I think you came not soon enough. *He stares after his mother, then shrugs the thought away.* Perhaps one should not expect, all within an hour, the habits of a lifetime to be changed.

A servant enters R. bearing two cups of wine on a tray. Pantites takes the cups and hands one to Geron. The servant bows quickly and departs.

Coming down C. with his cup. For me, life and death clashed with the percussion of brass cymbals, and in that moment was awareness born. Here — here death is the chipping of the mason's tool upon a monument — and life is just myself, her son, returned to wear a tunic she remembers. How could it be the same? *He drinks deeply from the cup.*

GERON — *Moving up C. and standing by the doorway, looking out into the street.* From here, which way lies the market place?

PANTITES — *Pointing the way.* Across the courtyard — to the right as you come upon the street.

GERON — At this hour, it will be crowded . . . And where do I find the taverns? — oh, not your kind; the dark dens where opinions brew and change hands across the counter . . .

PANTITES — Why do you want to know? Geron, you gave me your word that in Sparta at least, you would do nothing to embarrass me!

GERON — Always it is the same! Before the deed — suspicion; after it — a sermon. Since falling in with you, I am harrassed with morality! You have not forced honesty upon me — no; but you have made dishonesty so

37

complicated, I have almost lost my taste for it! *He puts down his cup, and holds out his hand to Pantites.* But let us not quarrel; I need you to finance a project.

> *Pantites sighs, and reluctantly takes out his purse, which he puts into Geron's hand.*

PANTITES   What project?

> *Geron opens the purse and peers into it, pretending not to hear.*

GERON   Did we earn all this upon the road? Amazing! Who would have thought there was so much profit in honest toil . . . ?

PANTITES   Geron — what project?

> *Geron looks out across the courtyard.*

GERON   I can see, crossing the courtyard, a gentleman whom I take to be your father . . .

PANTITES   *Looking out.* It is my father.

GERON   I thought so. There cannot be two men in Sparta today wearing that same aura of dilemma. So, your father comes — and I shall make my absence serve a double purpose.

> *He slips round the doorpost, disappearing.*

PANTITES   Geron — where can you be found, should I have need of you?

GERON   *Momentarily reappearing.* Should you need me, it will be my business to find you. *He vanishes.*

> *Pantites stands uneasily up C. watching his father approach. When Iolaus appears they greet each other nervously.*

IOLAUS   Pantites!

PANTITES	Father!

> *They hover awkwardly. They should embrace, but custom gives them no such outlet — so they stand with the feeling there, and no way to express it.*

IOLAUS	The news reached me at the City Hall — that the survivor was my son. I had to come — but I cannot stay. Your mother — ?
PANTITES	I have seen her.
IOLAUS	Yourself, Pantites — you are well? You have no serious wound?
PANTITES	No wound, Father.
IOLAUS	I saw a copy of your statement made to the Guard Commander, it is an incredible story . . . incredible! — or would be, were your integrity not so well known.
PANTITES	Surely no-one doubts my story?
IOLAUS	No — there can be no doubting the truth of your story . . . *His voice leaves a great deal unsaid, which plainly worries Pantites. Iolaus hastens to reassure him.* Pantites, before we go any further, let me reassure you at once, Cleon views our case with the utmost sympathy.
PANTITES	*Baffled.* Sympathy . . . ? Father, if I appear stupid, forgive me; I am a soldier, not a politician. If I am in some way at fault, I stand to be rebuked; but I cannot plead guilty until I know what I am supposed to have done!
IOLAUS	*After a long pause, uneasily.* Pantites . . . no-one, anywhere, has said precisely that you are at fault . . . No, no, but the situation is unprecedented — you must realise that. Cleon himself admits that he has not yet assimilated all its implication.
PANTITES	If there can be a situation to defeat Cleon's resources of definitive invention, it must be grave indeed! *His father gives him a sharp glance. Pantites prowls restlessly up to*

39

the window, then swings around. By a freak of chance I survive a battle in which my comrades perished; I return to Sparta with all promptitude, to report for further duty; tell me — for the love of Zeus! — where lies the fault in that? *Now really angry.* If any man discredits my story, let him charge me to my face!

IOLAUS   Pantites! Your impatience is understandable, and it has my sympathy. At the same time, I think you have more to gain by restraining your indignation, and showing the Elders that you are willing to co-operate in whatever they decide for you. Put your trust in Cleon. Though he has lost his own son in the battle, Cleon bears you no hostility.

PANTITES   Hostility . . . ? Cleon's son was my closest friend. —

IOLAUS   Exactly. As is his father mine. And it is Cleon's concern for me that prompts this deep anxiety to avoid the slightest trace of public scandal.

PANTITES   Father . . . have I in some unwitting way brought embarrassment upon the family?

IOLAUS   No, no, no — you misunderstand me. There is no personal embarrassment; but this city attributes to me a reputation, which, be it truly merited or not —

PANTITES   None but you, Father, would question that.

IOLAUS   — That is beside the point, we have to think not of what I am, but of what I represent.

PANTITES   *Softly, taken aback.* Does it mean no more to you than that?

IOLAUS   *Misunderstanding.* Oh, you need have no fear, Pantites; I shall make it my business to see that, whatever happens, you are accorded nothing less than justice.

PANTITES   I was not meaning that at all! You are the head of my family, and a highly-respected man of law, if I have cast a shadow upon you, personally, I will do anything you ask of me to mend the mischief. Anything! But if we are discussing that aspect of yourself which is merely

40

	a Spartan institution, and asking that in defence of that I should plead guilty to some crime still in the process of formulation — no! I find that I am growing hourly less reverent in my attitude to Spartan institutions!
IOLAUS	Pantites! Watch your tongue!
PANTITES	All seemed so simple when I left the battlefield . . . I thought only of returning home, of seeing my family again . . .
IOLAUS	*Embarrassed.* I cannot stay. I must discuss your case with Cleon. If you will prepare a statement for me, checking carefully on any details which you may have overlooked, we can agree between us the line of your defence.
PANTITES	You talk to me as a lawyer to his client — ! Father, it it too much that I should ask of you something more than legal guidance? *Once it is said, Pantites is as much embarrassed as his father.* I have said too much. Forgive me.
IOLAUS	*Pausing in the doorway, he chooses his words carefully.* Your recent experience would leave its mark upon any man — that we must all remember. *Iolaus bestows upon his son a brief, courteous smile — and thankfully makes his escape.*
	When Iolaus has gone, Pantites runs up C. to the doorway — then stops, defeated. He stares after his father, and then comes slowly down C. He is at a loss. A thought comes to him, which causes him to brighten for a moment. He runs up C. to the bell which he sets clanging violently. In answer to the imperious summons, three servants come hurrying upon the scene from R. and L. One carrying the tools he was using at the moment of interruption. They pause in a wide semi-circle and Pantites comes to stand in the centre of them, looking at each in turn.
PANTITES	*At length.* I do not know your faces . . . but I will have you, please, look well on mine. I am Pantites, son — and,

in his absence — master — of my father's house. At all times, you must answer to me everything with silence; that, I know, is the custom, and I like it not. You are men, equipped with a tongue that death can punctuate, at any moment, in mid-sentence. If that should happen, I should never have heard a voice from you, though we had shared beneath a mutual roof our fragile tenancy of time. So, when next I send for you, make me the offer of your name — or some comment upon the hour of day of condition of the weather. It is not eloquence I ask of you, but simply recognition. *He looks at them, they stare at him. To one of them briskly.* Hasten to the Palace of the Queen, and bear to my wife the news of my return.

> *The servant runs out C. Pantites exits L. The two remaining servants stare after him emptily.*
>
> *End of scene.*

The house of Iolaus. One hour later.

A table has been set in the centre of the hall. Servants bear in dishes from R. and L. and set them upon the table. Into the midst of this organised pattern of domestic activity, Pantites strays in from R. His battle-stained tunic has been replaced by one impeccably laundered. Pantites too, has been laundered — and looks in his elegance so miserably ill-at-ease that he might be inhabiting the body of a stranger. Seeing him, the servants, embarrassed by his recent gesture of equality, look at him uneasily, then concentrate upon their tasks — to fade from the scene as quickly as they can. Pantites is left alone in the presence of a table set for seven people. He looks about him, then, with a heavy sigh, slumps into a chair C. His attitude is one of complete dejection. Helena appears in the entrance C. from the street. She pauses, throwing back her veil — to reveal a young woman of some beauty.

HELENA   Pantites!

PANTITES   Helena! *He leaps to his feet — then pauses, uncertain now of his reception anywhere, but this time he has no cause to worry, for Helena runs joyfully into his arms.* Oh, Hera be thanked that there is one who welcomes me! *In his enthusiasm, the embrace sweeps her literally off her feet.*

HELENA   Pantites — put me down! It is not seemly in my mourning clothes.

PANTITES   *Laughs.* But you are not a widow now!

HELENA   *Rearranges her veil.* Oh no! — I am not — am I! But I wanted you to see that I'd mourned for you. Besides a veil is so becoming. *She laughs delightfully.*

Pantites tugs at her veil to remove it.

43

With a squeal. No! — Pantites! — you will disarrange my hair —

> *He pulls her again into his arms, kisses her — then pauses, looking past her face.*

PANTITES

Half to himself. There was a girl — at an inn upon the road — who made me think of you . . . *He recalls himself to the present. They embrace happily.*

HELENA

I saw your Uncle Hippias at the Palace — *She giggles suddenly and looks up to share the joke with him.* Since they made him Commander of the Palace Guard —

PANTITES

Surprised. Who — Uncle Hippias?

HELENA

Two months ago — had you not heard? Oh, wait until you see him! He takes himself more seriously now even than he did upon the field! *They both laugh happily over this.* They had sent word from the City Gate about you, and Uncle Hippias had in his hand a copy of that statement that you made —

PANTITES

Yet another copy? I wonder they have not had the City Crier publish it!

HELENA

I was just going to speak to him, and then — *She stops suddenly, realising that she does not really want to tell him the rest.*

PANTITES

Waits, wary now, but gentle. Go on.

HELENA

Troubled — then her face sets determinedly. It matters not. But . . . I wanted you to know — whatever they say about you — I am glad to have you home.

> *They embrace with feeling. They are more close in this moment, perhaps, than they have ever been.*

PANTITES

When you were so long in coming, I began to fear that your committee meeting mattered more . . .

HELENA

Pantites! No; the delay was not at the Palace, they withheld the news from me at first — not wanting to give me a second shock in my condition.

44

PANTITES   *Slow to grasp this at first.* Condition? What condition?
             Helena —

HELENA   *The awful truth hitting her.* Pantites — has no-one told
             you?

PANTITES   Told me? Told me what?

HELENA   *Moving from him.* Oh, they should have told you . . .

PANTITES   Told me what, Helena?

HELENA   *Pausing with her back to him.* I am going to have a child.

PANTITES   *Overjoyed.* Helena!
                    A brief pause.
             But I have been gone twelve months . . .

HELENA   Yes, Pantites.

PANTITES   *After a pause. Very quietly.* Who is the father?

HELENA   Oh, he comes from a very good family — his grandfather
             was a general.

PANTITES   *Thundering.* Who is the father?

HELENA   Pantites, do lower your voice! Do you want the servants
             to think we have àlready found a cause for bickering.

PANTITES   Dear heaven! *He turns away.*

HELENA   Oh, I can assure you, it was not my idea. The reasons
             were entirely patriotic.

PANTITES   *Comprehending.* Sons for Sparta? I see.

HELENA   And how do you think I feel about it? It is my figure
             that will be ruined. But I was given no choice. No-one
             knows how long the Persian War will last, and the Army
             is forever needing soldiers. So the Elders conferred, and
             the order was given for all Spartan women to start

breeding sons immediately. Those with husbands away at war, were told to find a substitute. *A silence.* Why take it so much to heart? You know the custom as well as I.

PANTITES   Yes. I know the custom. But need you have co-operated quite so efficiently?

HELENA   *Shocked.* Pantites!

PANTITES   You could have waited. You know that in a while I might return — or, if I died, you would almost certainly become a wife again.

HELENA   Pantites, you speak as if —

PANTITES   Who would have known, had you defaulted? Barren women are to be found in Sparta — none can force nature to co-operate unless she feels inclined. You were not obliged to acknowledge any man by name — and in the deed you were allowed a natural privacy. None could have proved you had not tried.

HELENA   *Amazed.* Pantites — what are you saying?

PANTITES   That you could have repelled the invasion of my marriage bed — had you been sufficiently inclined!

HELENA   *Outraged.* Anyone would think I had been unfaithful to you!

> Pantites just stares at her, lost for a reply to this one.

What choice had I? Would you, as a soldier, disobey an order? No — you would not think of it! And so it is with me.

PANTITES   Yes, but — dear heaven! — you cannot conceive a child with as little feeling as you order stores from the quarter-master!

HELENA   I had no personal interest in the man, if that is what you mean. Oh, I did show a little co-operation — that is only fair, I think. Besides, you would not want any man to tell another that Pantites had a frigid wife.

PANTITES	*Grimly.* I am sure you upheld the reputation of my marriage bed!
HELENA	I did my best. But when you start being jealous of him —
PANTITES	*Startled.* Jealous?
HELENA	You make the whole position quite absurd. I chose carefully a man whom I respect — indeed I could admit to liking him a little, and he has served his purpose . . .
PANTITES	And enjoyed it no doubt.
HELENA	But now you have returned. You are my husband, my place is with you.
PANTITES	Awaiting his child.
HELENA	It was my duty, Pantites. Do you, as a soldier question the order to kill?

He looks at her sharply.

	No, you would not dream of it. So it is with me. And of the two, you must confess, mine is the more constructive contribution. But I certainly do not love the man, or anything like that.
PANTITES	Helena. I think I should have preferred it if you had loved him.
HELENA	Pantites!
PANTITES	Yes, Helena! Love I understand; duty . . . I begin to wonder if I understand that at all.
HELENA	*She stares at him, then takes a step towards him. She tries to win him back to her.* You talk of love . . . and here we have been quarrelling since we met. *No reply. Her voice faltering.* You might at least remark upon my dress . . . It was chosen for you. Well — in respect of your memory, which is the same thing — I tried to wear a mourning dress you would have liked . . . *She is quite sincere in this, near tears.*

47

PANTITES	*Not hearing her.* And the others who fell at Thermopylae, are their wives breeding in the same way?
HELENA	It was a general order — to all women.
PANTITES	Love of Hera! Was it not enough to rob them of their lives, but they must needs be cheated, too, in their posterity! *He stands lost in his thoughts.*

> *Helena, trying to re-establish contact, makes a little gesture towards him, pathetic in its uselessness. Receiving no response at all, she turns, almost in tears, and hurries out L. Before she gives way to them. Pantites does not even feel her go. He stands C. in dark thought — then he moves in anger up to the window and stands looking out at the memorial.*

And you, my friends, whom they commemorate so heroically in marble — did you know they had made cuckolds all of you?

> *Geron appears in the doorway C. He sees the food and moves down towards the table.*

GERON	Ah . . . ! I hoped I should be back in time for dinner. *He moves along the table, glancing at each of the dishes with relish.* I was told it was the Spartan custom for gentlemen to dine in the public mess, and only the ladies ate their meals at home?
PANTITES	A Spartan family assembles round its own table on three occasions — weddings, funerals, and visitations of the plague. You can decide for yourself to which category I belong.
GERON	You have seen all the family?
PANTITES	I have seen them. *A pause. He eyes the table.* And I cannot decide if that funeral feast is set for me — or for them.
GERON	The dead should not come back — I told you.
PANTITES	Yes, you told me.

48

A pause.

Where have you been?

GERON

Well, while you have been grooming and garbing yourself . . . in a fashion, I might add, these three years extinct in Athens —

> *The disparagement causes Pantites to cast an involuntary downward glance at his attire.*

— I have put in a great deal of work on your behalf.

PANTITES

Distrusting him heartily. Such as?

GERON

Strolling round him, he tosses off the list. I have made known throughout the town the true facts of your history. I have been shaping for you a reputation as heroic as those terrible equestrian statues so beloved of your City Council . . . are they really the best that Sparta can do by way of modern art?

PANTITES

Eyeing him. Go on.

GERON

In other words, I have been making sure that the average Spartan citizen is likely to be on your side.

PANTITES

Puzzled. On my side? In what?

GERON

I am not yet sure, but as a student of military strategy, you should know that the successful opportunist does not leave everything to chance.

PANTITES

Worried now. Geron, what have you been up to?

GERON

You see? — you are not the least bit grateful!

PANTITES

I know your idea of an 'average citizen' and I have no wish to be sovereign of the stews and a brothel-darling here in Sparta!

GERON

A sigh. I can see you have a lot to learn! True, the men you want are those who think before they cast their vote; but they — alas — are the minority. The bulk of mankind is interested solely in its own advancement. It has to be bought — with promises. I have been buying it.

49

PANTITES	*More and more baffled.* What promises . . . ?
GERON	Oh, — profits here, wages there —
PANTITES	Geron —
GERON	— whatever, in fact, is the malocontents' personal vision of perpetual human happiness.
PANTITES	Geron —
GERON	It is standard political bait, Pantites — we are not talking about realities.
PANTITES	We are not talking about anything which is comprehensible to me!
GERON	In that case let us talk about something else —
PANTITES	*By now almost inclined to shake the truth out of him.* Geron — what have you been doing?
GERON	I have told you. And if you cannot yet see the reason for it, you should thank heaven for an accomplice with more foresight than yourself! *Sound of a dinner gong.* *Beaming.* Ah . . . dinner! *Melissa enters L. followed by a sulky Penthessilea.* *Penthessilea this time carries with her a scroll.*
GERON	*Bowing.* Madam . . .
MELISSA	*Looking anxious.* Geron, I must apologise for the lateness of the meal —
GERON	Why, then I am in better appetite!
MELISSA	— You see, it is such a rare event for the gentlemen to dine at home, I was not prepared . . . *Her voice tails off in embarrassment. She casts a quick glance at Pantites.*

50

Pantites, who has been studying his foot, glances up,
meets her eye, and turns away. This brings him to meet
the brooding, hostile gaze of Penthessilea from up L.
A hard look passes between them, then both simul-
taneously turn their back upon each other. This
brings Pantites back to face his mother — which leaves
Melissa fluttering a hand and rolling an eye as she
gropes for conversation. Your father sent a message, dear;
we are not to wait for him. *She turns to Geron.* My
hudsband is at the City Hall . . . Now, Geron, if you will
sit here on my right hand . . . *She moves up to the table,*
followed by Geron.

GERON   Your husband is a City Elder?

MELISSA   Oh, good gracious, no — he would not hear of it.

             Pantites moves to a place L.C. Helena enters
             quietly R. and Melissa rises to greet her with
             obvious relief.

MELISSA   Oh, there you are, dear . . . I am so glad, I thought you
             would be dining at the Palace — but, of course, with
             Pantites being home . . .

             Helena and Pantites turn to look at her.
             Melissa falters, then ends on a bright note.

With Pantites coming home, everything is different.
That she realises at once, was none too wise, either — so
she turns hurriedly to Geron. Do have some fish.

             Helena moves quickly down R. she and
             Pantites are now seated at the two opposite
             ends of the table. Melissa looks from one to
             the other and is seized with a sudden doubt.

With a gesture between the two of them. Have you
two . . . ?

PANTITES   Yes, mother. We have met.

             Helena and Pantites exchange a glance — not
             unkindly. Melissa, not knowing what to make
             of the situation, nods vaguely, and turns to
             Penthessilea — venting her exasperation.

51

MELISSA	Penthessilea, will you sit down — at once! — and eat your dinner.
	Her face tight in rebellion, Penthessilea comes to the table, selects a chair, and then sets it ostentatiously behind that of Pantites where she need not see his face. She sets down the chair with a thump — which causes Pantites to swing round angrily. They glare at each other — then Penthessilea flops, insolently, on her chair, and treats him to a long, contemptuous stare. This is too much for Melissa, who rises angrily and points towards the exit L.
MELISSA	Penthessilea, you have most adequately made your presence felt, and its social possibilities are now exhausted. Go to your room.
	Seething, Penthessilea rises. She glares at her mother, and then at Pantites, and then with a toss of her head leaves the table. Melissa recovers her social manner, and turns apologetically to Geron.
	And this before a guest — I blush for shame! Though you understand, perhaps, if you have growing daughters of your own —
	At this Penthessilea pauses on her way out, and turns, determined now to do her worst before she goes.
PENTHESSILEA	Yes, mother — let us blame it all upon my age!
MELISSA	Penthessilea!
PENTHESSILEA	Because I am fourteen, nothing I say need be taken seriously! And how fortunate that is for all of you.
MELISSA HELENA	Penthessilea! Will you be quiet?
PANTITES	Penthessilea — that will do!
PENTHESSILEA	*To Pantites.* To-morrow, what am I to tell the girls at school — ?
MELISSA	*To Pantites — rather helpless.* Pantites, pay no attention — it is her age . . .

PENTHESSILEA	*To her mother.* You did not say that of Pantites when Orlea called — !
MELISSA	Penthessilea!
PANTITES	*Sharply.* What is that?
MELISSA	Nothing dear. *She rises and goes to take Penthessilea by the arm.* Penthessilea, I think that you should go . . .
PENTHESSILEA	*Resisting her, she shouts the rest to Pantites.* Orlea called on her, when you were dressing. They should have gone together to the Queen's Reception this afternoon. But Mother is not entitled to go now, and Orlea was horrid about it —
MELISSA	*Trying to get rid of her.* Penthessilea —
PENTHESSILEA	— Because you have come back. Orlea was horrid to mother, because you have —

> *Melissa clasps Penthessilea's face against her in what seems to be an embrace, but which is in fact the only diplomatic way of stifling the tale. But it is too late.*

PANTITES	*Rising slowly.* Mother, what did Orlea say . . . ?
MELISSA	*Trying to cover up.* Orlea is an old friend . . . Old friends speak bluntly to each other. Naturally, she grieves much for the death of her son, and he has not returned. At heart she is bitter, and therefore must compensate . .

> *But there is really no way out of it — nor is there need to say more. Pantites comprehends. Melissa releases Penthessilea, for the damage now is done. In the pause which follows, there comes from outside the clatter of a horse's hoofs upon the cobbles, and the sound of a man's voice.*

HIPPIAS	*Off.* You, there — take my horse. Come along, man; quick about it.
MELISSA	*Now resigned to anything that can happen.* And here comes Uncle Hippias . . .

53

And Uncle Hippias it is, entering C. resplendent in full ceremonial uniform as Commander of the Palace Guard. Hippias is efficiency incarnate; he has never seen a joke, nor a major battle, in his life. His eye lights on Pantites and he comes straight down to him, his face worried.

HIPPIAS   Ah — Pantites.

PANTITES   *Coming to attention, a reflex action.* Sir.

HIPPIAS   Know what brings me here, of course? Bad business, this, nephew; bad business; very. Family like ours; tradition of gallantry in the field for evelen generations —

PANTITES   Twelve. Uncle, if you have read my statement —

HIPPIAS   Statement, yes; got it here. *He whips out a copy and scans it.* Tell you plainly, nephew — it worries me; worries me a good deal. You say here — "you thought you would be more use to Sparta alive . . ." what does it matter what you thought? — you had your orders. No place for private theorising in the Army; impairs efficiency. Give a soldier an order, keeps him happy; give him time to think, and where is he? — demoralised.

PANTITES   Uncle, it was after the battle I started thinking.

HIPPIAS   But why? Been given your orders; knew you should be dead; could have seized your sword and rushed the enemy.

PANTITES   *Patiently.* Uncle, the enemy had gone.

HIPPIAS   Well then, should have chased around. Persian scouting party? Soldiers themselves; understand your problem; relieved you of your life with pleasure.

> *Pantites lifts his hands to heaven in silent exasperation.*

No Persians? Last resort, do the job yourself; simple. Still, this is just between ourselves, Nephew — follow me? Make no accusations.

PANTITES   Frankly, I shall be happier when somebody does!

HIPPIAS	A soldier? Should need no telling. *With emphasis, slowly, for this is not merely a dictum.* Defeat becomes a triumph only when it can be said that the unit was annihilated to a man. The last man, Pantites. Follow me?
PANTITES	Yes, Uncle. And we were. Then I wakened up.
HIPPIAS	And that is what I mean! The Army does not recognise the condition of 'accidental survival'. It is your job to see that such a thing is not allowed to happen.
PANTITES	How?
HIPPIAS	That was your business. I have made enough suggestions. Damn it, you cannot be the first to be caught out this way; same thing must have happened to other fellows — dozens of 'em through the years: but we never heard about it. Follow me?
PANTITES	Yes, Uncle. My mistake would seem to lie in reporting back for duty. In order not to spoil the exercise, I should have gone absent without leave — or perhaps enlisted with the enemy . . .
HIPPIAS	Nephew! This is not the time for levity.
PANTITES	*His tone changing.* No — it is not! I have three hundred comrades dead of that same logic, and I start to wonder why!
HIPPIAS	Careful, nephew; that is treasonable talk.
PANTITES	Yes, Uncle. Forgive me. I am feeling treasonable.
	He turns away. In the momentary pause Iolaus enters C. He has about him an air of pleased success.
IOLAUS	Pantites, I have good news for you —
HIPPIAS	Iolaus — just a minute.
	To Pantites.
	Young man! Those who fell, they did not question their orders.

55

PANTITES	How do you know? They are dead!
	A pause.
	And I am asking, why are they dead? If there was a chance we could have held the Pass — yes, I could see reason in it. Or to occupy the enemy while the rest of our army got away — yes, there was reason in it. But to die as we did, needlessly, to achieve precisely nothing — !
HIPPIAS	Nothing! Nothing! The name of Thermopylae will ring forever down the ages —
PANTITES	As a supreme example of brave men giving their lives in a vain-glorious patriotic gesture!
HIPPIAS	How dare you, sir — !
PANTITES	Uncle, it was I who had to do the dying!
HIPPIAS	Then it was a pity you did not make a better job of it!
MELISSA	Hippias!
IOLAUS	Hippias, you address your sister's son . . .
HIPPIAS	Yes — my sister's son! Not content only to bring shame upon the family, he sets out now to disparage the heroism of his comrades — !
PANTITES	You talk of heroes; I talk of men — men I knew. Good fellows — good for sharing a joke or splitting a bottle; game to lie for a friend, or help chase a woman; and they are dead.
HIPPIAS	Dying is a soldier's job. Did they not teach you that at the Academy?
PANTITES	Yes, Uncle; upon a board, with wooden pegs plucked out and dropped into a box. I try still to see it that way — I do try! — but since Thermopylae the wooden pegs turn always into men — men! — trapped between the cliffs and the sea; three hundred pitched against six thousand — madmen, fighting like madmen, in a battle that they could not hope to win!

The original German production: Stadttheater, Rheydt —
Schönwiese, Goguel, Eickhoff.

Stadttheater — Rührdanz, Lorscheidt.

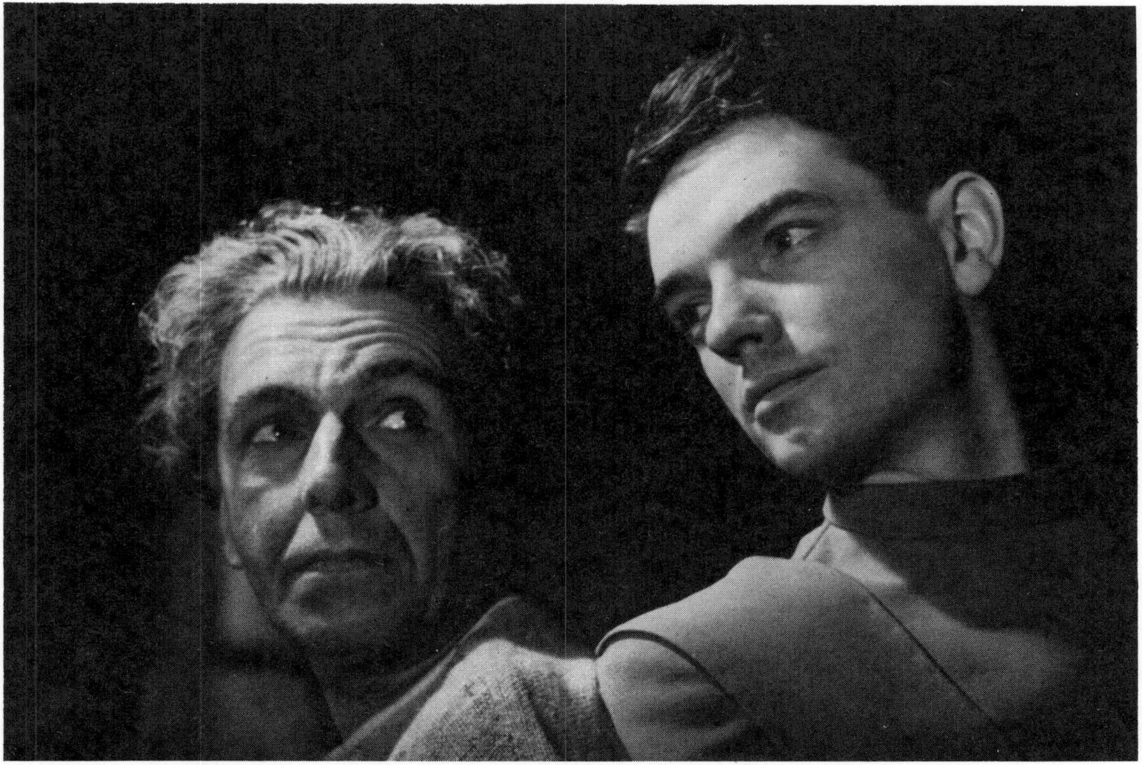

Stadttheater – Goguel, Lucht.

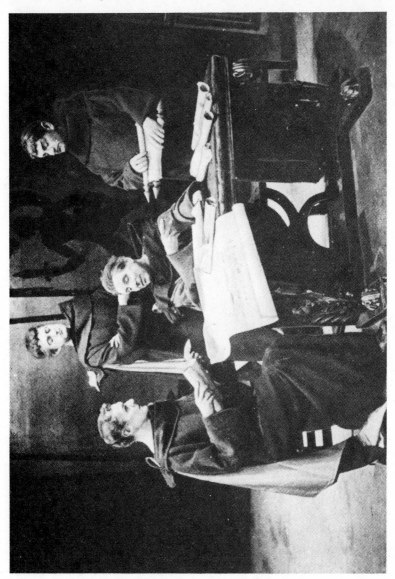

Edinburgh Gateway – Brown Derby, Martin Heller, James Gibson, Paul Kermack.

>   *Penthessilea, whom they have forgotten, has*
>   *crept nearer to follow the argument — and now*
>   *in her enthusiasm can no longer contain herself.*

PENTHESSILAE   *Ecstatically.* They say, on the eve of the battle they sat laughing and combing their hair . . . !

PANTITES   *Tossing it aside to her impatiently.* And what would you have us do — sit sweating and biting our nails?

PENTHESSILEA   *Suddenly flourishing her scroll.* Pantites, shall I read to you my poem?

MELISSA   Oh, not now, dear!

PENTHESSILEA   *Determined to have her say.* I have dedicated it — "To my Brother — Who Died at Thermopylae" —

PANTITES   Thank you very much. I can hear it later.

>   *He turns his back on her — but Penthessilea*
>   *rips into her poem.*

PENTHESSILEA   "Ye men, who here for Sparta lie
                   Proud in your robes of honoured death,
                   Beneath the gaze of reverent sky —
                   Forgive me that I still draw breath!"

IOLAUS   Penthessilea, that is quite enough.

PENTHESSILEA   *Who may as well defy everybody while she is about it.*
                   "Regard your wounds as hallowed scars;
                   Fairer than jewels, your sightless eyes:
                   What honour for you beneath the stars — "

MELISSA   Penthessilea!

PENTHESSILEA   " — Can match the joy of sacrifice."

HIPPIAS   That really is not bad at all — not bad at all.

PENTHESSILEA   "Though Sparta mourns, her tears are proud;
                   Greater than grief, her pride excels — "

57

PANTITES	*Rounding upon her with icy fury.* That will do, Penthessilea!
PENTHESSILEA	But —
PANTITES	That will do! *He snatches the scroll from her hands.* I have already had enough. I draw the line at a patriotic address from a child whose seat still bears the imprint of a schoolroom bench!
PENTHESSILEA	*Outraged.* Pantites!
PANTITES	Here — take away your wretched little poem and burn it! Show some respect for my dead comrades if you have none for me.
HIPPIAS	Pantites; I can make no sense of you; no sense at all. Had I been given your chance at Thermopylae, twenty years ago, when I was a young man . . . Would have died gladly —
PANTITES	Rubbish, Uncle!
HIPPIAS	— Gladly!
PANTITES	Rubbish! Whoever yet went into battle burning with a zest for death? You think only of life; of survival — of ending another man's life to save your own. Death is the enemy; the only enemy, whichever side you happen to be on.
HIPPIAS	If you put it that way, nephew — yes. You might remember I was facing death years before ever you were born.
PANTITES	Facing it, yes — and that, perhaps, is the difference. You have not been swallowed by it, and lain with it — and awakened with the smell of it upon you, to face it yet again. You have never been teased back to consciousness by the maggots foraging in your wounds — *As the ladies retract* — Yes! Death's corrosion is disgusting; that should be remembered when you send out men to die. And if we must die, let us have good reason for it. Who ordered the stand at Thermopylae, and why?

HIPPIAS	That is not for you to ask! You are a soldier; your King commanded you to die, is that not enough?
PANTITES	No, by heaven! — you shall not put the blame upon Leonidas! He was elected King and Commander — elected by the people of Sparta to represent their will. So it was your authority, Uncle Hippias — yours, Helena — yours, Mother —
MELISSA	Mine, dear? I had nothing to do with it.
PANTITES	No, you had nothing to do with it . . . I was condemned to death by all of you, but there is not one here who will own to it.
IOLAUS	*Stepping forward.* I will answer your questions, Pantites. No, Hippias — he is a Spartan citizen and has a right to know the reason.
HIPPIAS	Rights and reasons . . . !
IOLAUS	*To Pantites.* When the Confederacy sought our aid against the threat of Persian invasion, we could not afford a war on the scale anticipated by the other cities; nor could we, for the sake of our reputation, refuse to comply with the request. We agreed to send a token force. King Leonidas knew, before he left Sparta, that no more was expected of his men than some gesture to uphold Spartan military prestige, in that, they exceeded any duty that could have been asked of them.
	There is a respectful silence — broken by Pantites.
PANTITES	In other words, Sparta wanted her glory, but she wanted it on the cheap; we were to be sacrificed in the holy cause of this city's self-interest!
HIIPPIAS	Pantites, you have gone too far — !
PANTITES	Listen; I am a man and a Spartan. I will die to save another's life; I will die to save my wife from being raped and my children slaughtered; but — dear God! — to die for a reason such as you have given — !

PENTHESSILEA   *Ecstatically.* You died for Sparta!

PANTITES   Yes, Penthessilea — 'for Sparta'. And see what I owe
Sparta . . . ! When I was born, the Spartan Elders —
who had no part in my conception — examined my
head and my toes and the colour of my eyes, and
decided that I was healthy and Sparta could find a use
for me. Had one of my legs been shorter than the
other, I should — like my brother — have been left on
Mount Taygetos to die.

> *Melissa covers her face with her hands.*
> *Iolaus sees her.*

IOLAUS   Pantites, spare your Mother.

PANTITES   Did the state spare my mother? It took me from her
when I was seven years old, and put me into a barracks
school. There I was taught that there was no god but
the state, and no glory save in dying for it — or winning
the laurels at the Olympic games. At twenty, I was
allowed to marry, but still I was compelled to live in
barracks and see my wife by furtive visit — as if she
were some kind of secret vice the Army could overlook
but must not encourage! To crown my career, I was
packed off to die as part of an 'heroic gesture' — and in
my absence, Sparta, greedy for more soldiers made a
whore of my wife — !

HELENA   *Outraged.* Pantites!

PANTITES   *Angrily indicating the window* — And that is the
history not of myself alone, but of every single man
whose name on that Memorial you commemorate!

> *A pause.*

And because, through heaven's oversight, I commit the
error of surviving, I return to find —

IOLAUS   Pantites!

PANTITES   — To find that our 'heroic gesture' was no last ditch
defence of our homeland; it was a political device to
enhance Sparta's military reputation, and the slaughter
of three hundred of her citizens was the best and
cheapest way of doing it!

A pause. Very quietly

And that explains to me at last the 'crime' I have committed; I am the one who got away, the uneasy voice that asks too many questions.

PENTHESSILEA   *A wail as she runs from the room.* Oh, why could you not have died, Pantites? — I loved you as a hero!

                Her departure is unnoticed. They are all looking at Pantites.

                A pause.

HIPPIAS   Iolaus — this is serious. You are a magistrate; know your duty; have this man arrested.

PANTITES   That, Uncle, is the most useful contribution you have made!

IOLAUS   There is no law which forbids a young man to air a personal grievance at his father's table.

PANTITES   Father, you have my uncle here as witness . . .

IOLAUS   I told you, Pantites, that I brought good news. Cleon proposes to hold an informal enquiry by Council, and there is every hope that we can clear your name.

PANTITES   *Grimly.* I see.

IOLAUS   Upon one condition, Pantites; that you stand with your teeth tightly closed, and leave the oratory to me.

PANTITES   *Moving up to the window.* A little more conniving and invention at the City Hall, and I may well find myself being asked to unveil that eruption of pink marble in the square . . . !

HIPPIAS   Iolaus, is he referring to the Memorial . . . ?

PANTITES   *Swinging round.* And this is the process we call government! This is the mischief that we authorise when we elect our councillors! For the sake of municipal pride we send out men to die, then twist legal procedure

61

into knots to hide our subsequent embarrassment! *Indicating the window.* The average Spartan citizen — that man passing in the street — does he know what is done in his name by those elected to represent him? Does he know? If not, he shall be told!

HIPPIAS   *Appalled.* What? — rouse a rabble in the street?

PANTITES   If I am not to be allowed a voice at the enquiry, I must find a less sophisticated audience. Geron!

                   He moves to exit C.

MELISSA   *Frightened.* Iolaus — stop him! Cleon will show no mercy —

HIPPIAS   Treason! This is treason!

PANTITES   Yes, Uncle — treason! And if they send me to the gallows for it, I shall die this time in a worthier cause. But before I die, I swear to give truth such an airing that the towers of Sparta shall topple in the blast of it.

                   Pantites rushes out into the street, leaving behind him consternation. Geron, departs quickly and quietly in Pantites' wake.

                   End of Act One.

ACT TWO

SCENE 1

A room in the City Hall. One hour later.

Entrances R. and L. The Room up C. overlooks the city square — and the Memorial.

Cleisthenes sits pondering the scrolls which contain the Law of Sparta. Cleisthenes is very old and a little vague. Cleon stands by the window looking down into the square — from which rises the uproar of a mob being dispersed by the Civil Guard. The worst of the trouble is now past, and the noise gradually subsides — though the sound of a more quiet, orderly crowd is present throughout the scene.

CLEISTHENES   Under military jurisdiction, he could have been taken into custody upon a score of minor charges. Under Civil Law . . . apart from defaming the Government and its electors, and inadvertantly provoking a mob to violence, he has really done nothing — unless we charge him with Treason and Sedition, which you say you are not prepared to do. *He reaches for another scroll.* Ah, the city by-laws, now that may give us something . . .

SCORPIAS   *Enters breathless and indignant.* Such wanton destruction — I never saw its like! Half the masons' scaffolding torn down, and the column itself defaced with scribbled obscenities . . .

CLEON   What news of Pantites?

SCORPIAS   Pantites has disappeared. I asked everywhere for news of him, but no-one seems able, or willing, to give me further information. I am exhausted! *He flops on to a seat, fanning himself.* Of one thing I am sure, that crowd is not upon our side.

CLEON   *Watching from the window.* Their behaviour now is orderly. Too orderly. This is not the rabble that assaulted the Memorial; these are they who think before they come to make a crowd. *He turns and moves down C.*

65

SCORPIAS	*Rubbing his feet.* I saw many familiar faces. It is the usual varigated liberalism searching for an outlet. Or an organiser. *Rising.* I like not the way so many of the Council.are "indisposed" this afternoon, or engaged on business out of town.
CLEISTHENES	*Briefly, from his scrolls.* This. always happens when we have a crisis at the weekend.
CLEON	They are waiting to see which way it goes — like vultures, one eye closed, the other wide awake to opportunity.
CLEISTHENES	What about this . . . "The convening of an audience, planned or spontaneous, to witness any spectacle affording public entertainment upon unlicensed premises . . . ?
CLEON	The City Square is unlikely to be covered by a license.
CLEISTHENES	— "Premises requiring license:— taverns and tavern yards; brothels; amphitheatres; slaughterhouses; temple and temple precincts; markets (a) oovered, (b) uncovered.
CLEON	No mention of public squares?
CLEISTHENES	No, but I am not sure if the City Square can be defined in legal terminology as "premises". *Happily.* Iolaus will know! *Less happily.* Yes, Iolaus is sure to know . . .
SCORPIAS	Where is Iolaus?
CLEON	Did you not see him in the Square? He went down to hear his son's oratory, taking with him two council clerks to make a verbatim report of it.
SCORPIAS	He has been given leave to conduct his son's defence — that surely is enough without granting him further practical facility?
CLEON	It is in our own interest, no less than his, to have a detailed account of what Pantites said in his speech to the crowd — though, as most of it, from what I heard, placed the blame for our alleged misdeeds squarely upon

	the heads of the electors, I would be more inclined to give him our blessing than a vote of censure. As yet, I am afraid, we have no case against Pantites.
SCORPIAS	No case! *He gesticulates angrily towards the window.* The Memorial desecrated — and a dangerous mob assembled in the Square — what more must that young man do to qualify as a menace to our city?
CLEON	He must qualify within the letter of the law, which is quite a different matter.
CLEISTHENES	I have it!
CLEON	Yes, Cleisthenes?
CLEISTHENES	"Obstructing the public thoroughfare" — we have evidence enough that he is doing that. *He reads further and his triumph evaporates.* Oh . . . that applies only to chariots; handcarts; farmcarts; and all domestic vehicles, (a) wheeled, (b) unwheeled . . ." What is an un-wheeled vehicle, does anybody know?
SCORPIAS	*Crossing to Cleisthenes and taking up one of the scrolls. He glances over it — frowns.* Two days custody is all we need — time to pass a law making everything done by Pantites a capital offence.
CLEISTHENES	Would that be just?
SCORPIAS	*With a sardonic glance at Cleon.* It would be legal.
CLEISTHENES	*Rambling badly.* I wish it had been some one other than Pantites . . . Of all the boys who robbed my orchard, he was the only one who remembered to shut the gate . . .
SCORPIAS	*Reading from the scroll* . . . "Nocturnal brawling" — "Drunkeness" — "Obscene language in the Temple" — "Leaving litter in the Park" — *He hurls the scroll back on to the pile.*
CLEON	Nothing! Not one charge upon which we could hold him for an hour.

Iolaus enters quietly R. seen by Cleon.

67

Nothing, Iolaus! Not one law your son has broken . . . !

IOLAUS	As a father, I am gratified to hear it. As a magistrate pledged to guard the peace of this city, I am appalled.
CLEON	You have Pantites' words recorded?
IOLAUS	Yes; a copy will be brought to us presently. I am afraid that will not be much help to you, either. He lectured the crowd on the theme of moral responsibility — a subject so far removed from any political party agenda, that it disqualifies him instantly as a candidate for government.
CLEON	*With interest.* Did anybody listen?
IOLAUS	No. They were so busy shouting 'Pantites for King!' they drowned almost everything he said.
SCORPIAS	*Shaken.* King!
IOLAUS	Oh, they will be shouting for his head tomorrow. By the time I left, they were already switching their allegiance to a lout on the front row who made more noise than the rest.
CLOEN	And Pantites?
IOALUS	He is somewhat disillusioned.
SCORPIAS	It was he who instigated the assault on the Memorial.
IOLAUS	On the contrary, when he realised what was happening, he made a courageous attempt to defend it against the mob.
CLEON	Where is Pantites now?
IOLAUS	Presumably, continuing his search for honest citizens. He asked me where they might be found.
CLEON	So you did speak with him?

IOLAUS	I told him he would find the honest citizens at home, engaged in the business of being honest.
CLEON	*Going up to the window and glancing out. With a sigh.* Apart from the optimistic few who will join any ideological caravan that seems to be going part way in the right direction . . . !
SCORPIAS	Which brings us back to the beginning. We shall have to charge him with Treason and Sedition.
CLEON	Impossible.
SCORPIAS	There is no alternative.
IOLAUS	Upon the Treason and Sedition charge, he must be tried in open court and given the opportunity to defend himself.
CLEON	— Letting him air in public his own views on the Persian campaign. No!
SCORPIAS	I cannot see that matters — providing the trial results in his conviction.
CLEON	Conviction — acquittal — it is the process of the trial which will be damaging.
SCORPIAS	To us?
CLEON	To our city. Have you forgotten by what small majority we turned the Council vote to favour war?
SOCRPIAS	Subsequent events have proved you right.
CLEON	Subsequent events have merely proved, yet again, that a natural reverence for the courage of dead men will silence the haggling of rival factions — for a while. If we bring Pantites to trial on a charge of Treason, we shall break that armistice. Do you think Pantites' is the only voice that will be heard? All the professional critics will be there, clambering aboard the platform to enjoy a banquet of recrimination!

There is a pause. Cleon moves away. Scorpias frowns in thought.

SCORPIAS

I suppose there is no way that we can try him upon the Treason charge . . . secretly?

IOLAUS

None.

SCORPIAS

It has been done.

IOLAUS

Not within our time.

SCORPIAS

Iolaus, we realise that you are fighting for the life of your son, but —

IOLAUS

I am demanding justice for one anonymous Spartan citizen.

SCORPIAS

Oh come now, is there a father or a son in Sparta who will believe that — ?

CLEON

I am a father — *He breaks off. Flatly.* I was a father. And I believe it.

SCORPIAS

We have to make some allowance for human nature.

IOLAUS

Impatiently. This, Scorpias, is one occasion when no allowance can be made for human nature. Can you not see? — it is the law of Sparta which is on trial today, not Pantites. The fact that the young man in question does happen to be my son draws the more attention to ourselves and our handling of the affair — it certainly lends nothing to his advantage, for we dare show no clemency. But justice he must have. I seek not to prove his innocence; I am demanding that you establish lawfully his guilt.

SCORPIAS

Angry. The situation is preposterous! Is the Council to be held to ransom by the argument of a mere magistrate?

CLEON

That "mere magistrate" my friend, is a man whose reputation for integrity towers above this city like a white obelisk. Let some mischance overtake Pantites,

70

	and Iolaus will have the entire Council of Elders put on trial for murder.
SCORPIAS	He would not dare!
CLEON	Oh, he would dare; I do not say he would succeed, but the attempt would be enough to unseat the government.
SCORPIAS	*Drawing Cleon aside out of hearing of Iolaus and lowering his voice.* Then I am driven to suggest . . . could we not arrange for the son's fate to embrace simultaneously the father . . . ?
	Cleon regards him a moment pensively, faced with the problem of trying to explain.
CLEISTHENES	*Despite his vagueness and apparent hardness of hearing, he has contrived to hear every whispered word of this.* Bless my soul! — what is the Council these days coming to? It is all these young Elders . . . *He glares at Scorpias from beneath his wispy brows.*
CLEON	No government can live by honesty alone; that is accepted. But in so far as we can, we must deal honestly — and not solely for reasons of altruism; as every tyrant has found, oppression is a limited convenience.
SCORPIAS	I think you will find, when all ways else have failed.
CLEON	When all ways else have failed — yes. In no case otherwise. To ensure the survival of Sparta I will do absolutely anything; but I will not undertake lightly any piece of moral surgery that will diminish Sparta.
	He moves away.
	Hippias arrives suddenly in their midst.
HIPPIAS	Cleon! Something must be done — at once — to restrain this — this — rogue soldier; creating chaos; scandalous. Less than twenty minutes ago; appeared on horse at the Palace Gate, demanding audience with the Queen — !
SCORPIAS	*Horrified.* Uninvited?

71

HIPPIAS	And on the day of her Reception — with the mothers and widows assembled!
CLEON	Was he admitted.
HIPPIAS	*Unheeding.* — Came galloping across the park, ignored the sentry, jumped three flower beds, and addressed me as "Uncle" in front of the men. Not good enough, that sort of thing.
CLEON	Did he see the Queen?
HIPPIAS	No idea. A Spartan citizen; within his rights; had to admit him. Handed him over to the Chamberlain. No idea what happened after that — too embarrassed to enquire. This time I am insisting, Cleon — insisting! — somebody must take action. If you cannot find a solution here in the City Hall, you must let the Army handle it.
SCORPIAS	Out of the question!
HIPPIAS	Why? No problem to us. Arrest him for mutiny. Simple.
CLEON	*Still calm, but thinking fast.* There must be no court martial.
HIPPIAS	At least he would get a fair trial, which is more than he is likely to get from you!
IOLAUS	Hippias, there will be justice done. You have my word on that. So long as it remains within my power to guarantee it.
	On this, said quietly, the eyes of Iolaus meet those of Cleon for a moment. There is in the stillness of Iolaus now a sense of possible, though not yet certain, doom.
HIPPIAS	Is it justice to deny the lad his rights? He is a soldier, entitled to a cell in the barracks, army rations and an escort guard of equal rank. Treating him like a damned civilian — it is scandalous, Cleon. Scandalous. But something must be done at once. If you will not act with sufficient authority, I shall.

72

He goes out briskly.

CLEON   *Thinking aloud.* He must be taken by the Civil Guard —
               at once . . .

IOLAUS   Upon what charge?

CLEON   Does it matter — now? Pantites will be the victim of
               too many champions. Everyone sees in that young man
               some aspect of himself. His appeal is not to reason, but
               to emotion. You cannot ask for him the impartiality
               of justice; it is my duty to protect the law.

               End of scene.

A quiet corner of the city. Half an hour later.
Pantites sits, dejected, in the shadow of a wall.
Geron enters.

GERON   Ah, — there you are! I have been searching everywhere.

PANTITES   I have been at the Palace.

GERON   So I heard.

PANTITES   I thought the widow of Leonidas and the bereaved ladies gathered round her might turn a more attentive ear to my suggestion.

GERON   Which was?

PANTITES   The official demolition of that memorial.
                    Geron sighs.
I still think that if the citizens were to see the humbling, stone by stone, of that monument to civic pride they might read from it an altered patriotic disposition.

GERON   And did the Queen agree to your suggestion?

PANTITES   No! The Queen, like any other Spartan citizen, does not want to know! She loved her husband and her grief is real, but, like the rest, she values her sleep and prefers to hang the blame for his death upon that marble scapegoat in the City Square.

GERON   I have told you you will not raise a conscience in this city.

PANTITES   Yet, I must try. I have three hundred comrades dead; three hundred times myself, within myself, crying to be heard.

GERON   And do you suppose they, beyond the Styx, care one

quarter for your dreadful dedication? Being out of it, I am sure they have far more sense than to let our world's half-baked values wreck their sleep.

A pause.

So you have given up your search for honest citizens?

PANTITES   Honest citizens! The mob in the Square is bad enough, but you should have been with me at the Palace! There was not a corner where there did not lie in wait for me some potential politician lusting for advancement. I did not know that Cleon had so many enemies.

GERON   And you rejected every offer?

PANTITES   Do you think I want my cause embraced for any but the rightful reasons?

GERON   In your predicament, you should welcome any ally. You, my friend, are in trouble. The guard has been doubled on all the city gates, and there are six platoons — four civil and two military — competing for the privilege of arresting you.

PANTITES   *Cheered by this.* Upon a charge of treason?

GERON   No. For riding a horse across the Palace Flower Beds.

A pause.

PANTITES   My father warned me that Cleon was in a mood to be inventive. . .

GERON   We must secure your safety somehow. Have you any money?

PANTITES   No.

GERON   *A bright thought.* Can we sell the horse?

PANTITES   Horse? *He remembers.* The horse was borrowed.

GERON   And you returned it? Oh — ! How can you have so little foresight. *He despairs of him.* Now we are lacking

76

both the means to leave the city and the means to stay. *He stands frowning for a moment then glances at the wall. He goes to peer over it.* What have we here . . . ? Ah . . . a garden, large, deserted, and profusely planted out with trees . . .

PANTITES   Geron! You are spying on the temple precincts.

GERON   Am I . . . ? *He rubs his hands cheerfully.* Now could we have a better piece of luck . . . ? The very place where no-one is likely to go looking for you.

> *A sound of men and horses from the distance. Geron shows sudden urgency.*

Pantites — make haste! There is a search patrol coming this way.

> *As Pantites sits in thought, making no move.*

Pantites!

PANTITES   *Coming suddenly to life, having reached a decision of his own.* I have other business.

> *He rises and turns to go in the opposite direction.*

GERON   *Plaintive.* Are you mad?

PANTITES   I am going to the City Hall.

GERON   You go to meet death, Pantites.

PANTITES   *A slight smile.* We are old acquaintances.

> *Pantites makes his exit. Geron looks after him, then departs hurriedly his own way, towards the temple, as the sound of the search patrol approaches.*

End of scene.

The City Hall. Some minutes later.

Iolaus sits alone at the table, writing. Calmly he pauses now and again to consider what he writes. Cleon enters quietly, and stands for a moment watching him. Then he comes forward.

CLEON   Working, Iolaus?

IOLAUS   I must prepare my son's defence.

CLEON   *Harshly.* He will not need it.

IOLAUS   I shall continue to prepare it.

CLEON   Iolaus . . . before the others come — is it not possible to resolve our differences by a compromise?

IOLAUS   Let me hear the proposition.

CLEON   To save you — for Sparta — I will run part way with the law. Pantites shall be charged with Treason. I will appoint the day for trial, let it be known that you are engaged in his defence — I do not claim for the plan originality!

IOLAUS   Well?

CLEON   — Upon the eve of trial, men have been known to choose suicide in preference to immeasurable risk. There is usually found beside them a confession, written and signed by their own hand —

IOLAUS   I see why you do not claim originality!

CLEON   In this case, I will make one small innovation of my own. His "confession", when published, will be phrased to suggest that he chose death to spare our city the distress of further controversy. Thus will he be remembered not as a coward but as a man of honour.

IOLAUS	A generous offer.
CLEON	Then you will agree?
IOLAUS	To what?
CLEON	Merely to hold your tongue.
IOLAUS	Is that possible?
CLEON	*Harder now.* Iolaus, if you persist in demanding trial for your son —
IOLAUS	That is the law of Sparta. We cannot change it to suit political convenience. My son is innocent until he is found guilty by just and impartial trial.
CLEON	For some men justice happens merely to be impossible. And if you, Iolaus, continue to press for it, you will not save your son, and you will almost certainly destroy yourself. *Urgently now, he comes to plead with Iolaus.* Iolaus, I am asking you to think of Sparta. Can the rights of one superfluous young man be measured against those of a hundred citizens who look to you for justice?
IOLAUS	Deny justice to one man, and what guarantee of it have the other ninety-nine?
CLEON	But if we can preserve the aspect of justice? Surely for that you might think it once a better thing to hold your tongue? No-one need ever know that you had compromised.
IOLAUS	You would know.
CLEON	I recognise the need for expediency.
IOLAUS	Which is why you value me — because I have never recognised it. If you corrupt me, Cleon, I should be of no more use to you. *He rises suddenly, by far the more powerful of the two.* Cleon, you made me what I am. To be simply a magistrate, interpreting the law as honestly as I could — that would have contented me; and as a private citizen, to live within the compass of my own

integrity. But that was not enough for you. We must have in Sparta, for all eyes to see, a monument to justice — and his name shall be Iolaus, surnamed the Just . . . so you created me. But you have made me too well; now, to preserve your monument, you must submit to it — or see it destroyed.

CLEON *In anguish.* Iolaus . . . Iolaus, you cannot win. However well and hard you fight, you cannot win!

IOLAUS *Serene.* No, Cleon — I cannot win. But our sons did not make their stand at Thermopylae with any hope of winning.

>*There is a pause. Then Pantites enters quietly R.*

>*Seeing him. With a rare note of welcome in his voice.* Pantites . . . !

>*Pantites meets his eye with curiosity — then a half smile of recognition passes between them.*

PANTITES Greetings, father . . .

>*He turns to Cleon.*

Cleon, I hear you have been seeking me. To spare you further trouble, I have come to you.

CLEON *Taking him by the hand, he is quite sincere.* Pantites . . . Pantites, this meeting has been too long delayed. You should have come earlier, it would have spared us both much embarrassment. But this is not time to be wasted in recrimination; what have you in mind that brings you here to see me?

PANTITES Nothing. That is why I came to you. I am eager for suggestions.

CLEON *A load of anxiety departing from him.* Well, then we can save ourselves a whole world of anxiety! *He is warm towards Pantites, and gives Iolaus a look of relief. Iolaus, who knows his son, is more inclined to fear the worst.* Pantites . . . can we not turn back the page, and see you again as you arrived this morning at the City Gate — one surviving soldier dutifully returned to report to his commanding officer?

PANTITES *Grimly.* Go on.

81

CLEON	*Still persuasive, but less optimistic.* There must be a second expeditionary force despatched to meet the Persians and who is better fitted to command it than yourself?
PANTITES	Upon what terms? That I redeem my honour by dying ferociously in the next engagement?
CLEON	That is the soldier's traditional privilege.
PANTITES	It is the traditional privilege of a soldier who has been accused, tried, and convicted of cowardice!
CLEON	The choice is yours, Pantites.
PANTITES	Choice — when there is but one alternative? *A pause.* And if I do have the good fortune, this time, to die . . . what will happen to my name inscribed on that memorial?
CLEON	Orders have already been given for your name to be erased. Pantites, you could have remained with the dead and none been the wiser — it was you who threw away your chance to share their immortality —
PANTITES	Immortality! Their immorality would seem to lie not in being heroes but in being dead!
CLEON	*Growing angry.* Pantites! That is enough!
PANTITES	No — you cannot see it, can you? You will go on building your monuments, flaunting your pride in the teeth of every city-state in Greece; you will shout 'Thermopylae' until prosterity is deafened with the name! They are your heroes! But . . . let one of those three hundred show his face at the City Gate tomorrow, and you will give him the self-same reception you have given me.
CLEON	That is enough — ! Enough!
PANTITES	And that is why, upon some pretext —

82

CLEON	Enough — !
PANTITES	— Any pretext, you must have me dead! So be it; but in furtherance of your plan you need not look to me for co-operation. No, Cleon! I will not die a second time to suit political convenience.
CLEON	*Controlling his rage.* Iolaus, there is nothing to be gained by trying to reason with this man. He must be silenced.
PANTITES	Cleon, so long as there is life in me, I cannot hold my peace. Nor in death — for death will free my voice to cry forever at the heels of time, damning the legend in its protest. And that is the only action left to me — to confound you with the problem that I am.
CLEON	Iolaus, you demand justice for this man; he shall have it. Beneath the prison, there is an ancient dungeon used now as a charnel pit; into it he shall be thrown, with food enough and water to last him twenty years. He shall be returned, alive, to the dead with whom he belongs. Can you say that is not justice!
IOLAUS	Cleon!
PANTITES	I am in your hands, Cleon!
IOLAUS	*Turning upon them both.* In the name of Zeus! Must I be obliged to keep the peace between two madmen? Cleon, I know the deeper cause whereby you are inflamed, but you speak for Sparta, and in our politics we do not allow the intrusion of personal animosity. Pantites, you are like all young men blinded by their first vision — you cannot see that your lust for martyrdom is as destructive as any of the forces you condemn. You are not fighting dragons, you are encumbering old men who have to keep the peace in this ungrateful city. Do you think you are the first to see that society is not all it should be? Do you imagine that you voice a challenge never heard before? Forty years ago, Cleon and I outburned the dawn with our theories . . . truth and liberty we promised to the earth, and truth and liberty was our intention . . . *Sad and a little sardonic, he turns away.*

PANTITES	And . . . what happened?
CLEON	Happened . . . ?

> *The two older men look at each other,*
> *baffled for a moment by the question — then*
> *they remember that he does not know.*

It happened . . . as it always happens.

IOLAUS	And if at the end of it, Pantites, you have still enough respect for truth and justice to think of embalming its corpse — well, you have survived the race better than most.

PANTITES	*Shocked.* Father! — you have no need to echo Cleon's cynicism; as long as there is one man in this city whose integrity survives . . . *His voice fades as thought shapes itself uneasily.* Cleon . . . is that the reason why you have always opposed any attempt to elect my father to the Council?

IOLAUS	*His voice flat in its bitterness.* And if the Council contemplates some measure which Cleon knows my 'integrity' will be obliged to challenge, he keeps from me — until it is too late — all knowledge of it . . . !

PANTITES	*To his father.* And you know of this? That your integrity — that impeccable integrity — is leased to you, subject to revision, by grace of Cleon's patronage?

> *Iolaus looks at him, his face empty. Then*
> *moves away.*

CLEON	Yes! — if you insist upon the truth; Iolaus the Just is a legend — a legend false as the painted masks that hang upon the temple wall; but without such legends, what should we have to strive for, higher than ourselves? *In sudden anger.* This we have given to our city — in a lifespan twice the length of yours! And now you, Pantites, in your youth and your arrogance and your stupidity, threaten to destroy it! What manner of hazy virtue are we supposed to see in that? And if you do destroy it, what better have you to offer in its place?

> *Pantites stares at them both silently. The*
> *stillness is broken suddenly by the entrance of*

	a Priest. Cleisthenes and Scorpias tag at his heels. The Priest is breathless with running, and in a state of frenzy that is half ecstasy, half terror.
PRIEST	Cleon! Cleon! I have seen a god!
	They regard him in astonishment. The Priest throws himself upon the floor.
	I have seen a god! I have seen a god! Oh — I have seen a god — !
	He sways wildly on his knees, repeating the statement over and over again. They watch him, rather at a loss — Cleisthenes and Scorpias grouping, themselves with the others.
CLEISTHENES	Oh, dear, dear . . . poor fellow! Some kind of fit, I daresay . . .
CLEON	*Sharply, to the Priest.* Very well — you have seen a god; as a Priest that is an occupational hazard for which you should be prepared.
PRIEST	*Shocked, he stops babbling and sits back on his heels more sensibly.* Yes, but it was a real god — not one of ours.
CLEISTHENES	'Not one of ours' . . . what does the fellow mean?
PRIEST	A god — with my own eyes I saw — standing on the altar.
SCORPIAS	Standing — on the altar? Irreverence!
IOLAUS	*To the Priest.* My friend — who was the god?
CLEON	Iolaus, does it matter? Let the Temple deal with its own problems — we have enough on our hands.
PRIEST	The Seventh Choral Ritual had just ended. Two of us had stayed behind to tidy up the sanctuary. I was on my knees, dusting the sacrificial ash from Castor's plinth — and then it happened!
CLEON	What happened?

PRIEST	The light began to fade — through no hands had touched the candles — and a darkness came upon us, such a darkness as must have been the night before the world began. Then came the wind — a great, great, wind . . . The walls of the sactuary groaned, caging a hurricane — yet we felt nothing, not one hair upon my head was moved. And then — he was suddenly there, upon the altar, in a blinding radiance of light . . .

He bows his head, for a moment forgetting his audience in the memory of it.

CLEON	Who was — ?
PRIEST	Hermes, himself — Hermes, Messenger of the Gods — and I with these same eyes, the duster in my hand, and my eyes were level with his feet. I saw the wings at the heels of his sandals . . . fashioned of tiny feathers, such as you find upon a sparrow — but these were white, shining white like goose feathers, but whiter than any goose I ever saw . . . *He smiles to himself at the memory.*
CLEON	And did — Hermes — have anything to say for himself?
PRIEST	He brought a message from the Gods.
SCORPIAS	To Sparta — to us? Oh, wait till the other cities hear of this!
PRIEST	'Go to the City Hall' — he told me — 'and say to them that are assembled there' — I give you his very words — 'say to them, that he who has returned from the dead, was spared by the will of heaven, and must be allowed to go safely about whatever business he may choose. Any man who dares to check him, will be called upon that very day to answer for the deed before the throne of Zeus.' *There is a deathly hush.* His message delivered, he mounted again upon the wind, and was swallowed into darkness. The altar candles bloomed into flame, and we were alone in the stillness of the sanctuary.

Stricken speechless, Pantites takes a step towards the Priest and then stops. The others turn slowly to stare at Pantites. The Priest throws himself at the young man's feet, kissing them.

86

PRIEST   Holy Young Man, I am your servant. Command me as
                you will, it shall be done —

PANTITES   *Repelled, he tries to step back.* No!

PRIEST   *Clinging to his feet.* Anything, Holy man — anything! —
                whatever you command — it shall be done —

PANTITES   *Breaking free of the Priest's embrace.* Leave me! Leave
                me!

                    *The Priest, dismissed, rises and backs out of
                    Pantites' sight — then he turns and runs out.
                    There is a hush. Pantites retreats from them
                    to the corner up L. where he stands with his
                    back to them, his face pressed to the wall and
                    his arms covering his head. Iolaus creeps like
                    an old man to the table, and sits behind it,
                    his head in his hands. Cleon's control gives
                    way suddenly. He raises his arms to heaven in
                    a roar of exasperation.*

CLEON   Oh . . . ! As if life were not difficult enough, without
                interference from the gods!

                    End of Act Two.

ACT THREE

SCENE 1

The City Hall. Two minutes later.

Pantites and Iolaus are positioned as we left them. Cleon is striding wrathfully to and fro, trying to think his way out of the situation, with Scorpias and Cleisthenes edging helplessly after him, twittering suggestions.

SCORPIAS   There is always bribery, of course . . .

CLEON   And whom do we bribe this time — the gods?

SCORPIAS   Everywhere, there is always someone who can be bribed. Among the priests, there is a —

CLEON   Scorpias, the Temple has for centuries claimed authority on behalf of heaven, with not one shred of evidence to show for it. Do you imagine they will let anything stop them exploiting a revelation like this? *To himself.* A trick, it must be a trick — but how, and by whom? *He stops and looks across at Pantites.* If we can convince the populance that it is a trick, Pantites can be burned at the stake for blasphemy.

CLEISTHENES *Shaking his head.* Nasty business, blasphemy . . .

             Cleon resumes his pacing.

SCORPIAS   *Terrified.* Cleon — think of the risk! We have just been warned, by Heaven, that boy is untouchable.

CLEON   You saw the priest prostrate before him; how long do you think it will be before we have the entire population of the city on its knees, imploring his favour?

CLEISTHENES *Nodding to himself.* And to think he used to raid my apple trees . . . ! Do you think my orchard will become a holy place, visited by pilgrims? Perhaps I ought to build a shrine there . . . Oh, just think of it — all my little marrows will be hallowed . . .!

CLEON	*To Scorpias.* You see? And you, Scorpias — would you make a stand against the boy's omnipotence?
SCORPIAS	*Alarmed.* On no account! I wash my hands of the whole affair. It is all very well for you — you are an atheist.
CLEON	I should need proof to sway me either way. But one thing I do know, without wanting proof, no city can afford to have within its boundaries a man who is answerable only to heaven.

> *From afar, comes the sound, very faintly, of music and the noise of the crowd beginning to gather again in the square. Cleon goes to the window glances down. He pauses thoughtfully, then turns sharply to the others.*

	This is a matter which must be debated in privacy. Cleisthenes — Scorpias.

> *He shepherds them towards the exit R. then turns as Iolaus addresses him.*

IOLAUS	Cleon. Cleon, if you have any plan at all, I will support you.
CLEON	He must die.
IOLAUS	It is the only way.
CLEON	And you will not demand justice for him?
IOLAUS	How can I demand justice for a man who is above justice?
CLEON	*Slight smile.* I knew at the end you would be the only one.

> *He takes Iolaus by the arm, and they make their exit R. after the others.*
>
> *Pantites has turned during this last exchange, and now he comes some way down C. to stand looking after them.*
>
> *The sound of music can now be heard quite plainly — cymbals, harps, pipes, and drums, united in joyous vigour if in nothing else.*

	Despite his dejection, Pantites' curiosity grows too much for him. He moves up to the window. As he looks out, he is sighted by a few members of the crowd in the square — who promptly begin to cheer. Pantites steps back hastily out of sight. Geron appears L.
GERON	Psst! Psst!
	Pantites turns.
	You are expected at the Temple.
PANTITES	At the Temple?
GERON	There are sixteen priests, fourteen youths and maidens, nine musicians, six little girls with garlands, seven sacred cows, four baskets of doves, and — quite independently — one small boy with a trumpet — all waiting for you in the street outside.
PANTITES	What?
GERON	To escort you to the Temple.
	As Pantites looks at him blankly.
	Well, you might at least come and wave your hand to them or something — at the moment they are holding up the traffic.
PANTITES	Geron — you did this!
GERON	Did what?
PANTITES	I thought this business at the Temple smelled to heaven of your handiwork.
GERON	*Glancing about him with satisfaction.* Well, you must admit, Hermes himself could not have dispersed your enemies more effectively.
PANTITES	But what have we achieved by it? I am still to die.
GERON	Well, we have saved your father.
PANTITES	*Startled.* My father?

PANTITES	*Baffled.* But, less than a moment ago, I saw my father go out with Cleon — discussing how best to dispose of me . . .
GERON	And what choice had he? None. Which puts him safely out of danger. But we are wasting time. You keep the procession waiting.
PANTITES	You are not expecting me to take part in this impious carnival?
GERON	Do you think I have arranged it all for nothing? It is the safest way of getting you to the Temple. The High Priest will give you full board and sanctuary — he can do no less, considering the custom you will bring to his neglected institution. Secure within the Temple, you can issue an edict — dissolving the Government of Sparta, annulling the Constitution, and vesting all authority in your own person. And if there should be any resistance, I shall be at hand with enough lightning, thunderbolts and headless horsemen to put the fear of heaven into Zeus himself. Thereafter the field is yours — though you would be well advised to lose no time in putting down Cleon and the others. You can throw them into prison — or make a thorough job of it, and have them done to death. I recommend the latter course myself.
PANTITES	*Who has been staring at him silently. His words come slowly.* You are not joking, are you?
GERON	*Slapping him cheerfully on the shoulder.* This is no time to show dejection! Power, my friend — limitless power! — that is what I have given you.
PANTITES	Power . . .
GERON	The world is yours, boy — yours! — as Zeus has it — resting like a marble in the hollow of his hand.
PANTITES	*Sickened.* And what am I supposed to do with it?
GERON	Why, put the world to right! Bring to the earth peace, and justice and charity . . . you must agree, they have long been overdue.

GERON	Yes. Had you not realised?
PANTITES	And charity begins today in Sparta — with the indiscriminate massacre of the City Council.
GERON	*A shrug.* No victory is won without casualties.
PANTITES	*Grimly.* And after the Council, who will be next? I can tell you now — my father. He must die because he will take Cleon's part, as he earlier took mine.
GERON	Pantites, you must learn to be a man of vision. Every Golden Age is preceded by a purge.
PANTITES	"Every" Golden Age?
GERON	Now, now — cynicism does not become you. You are an honest man, of good intention.
PANTITES	So was Cleon in his day. I can believe it now.
GERON	*A pause. A sigh.* You will not do it?
PANTITES	It cannot be done.
GERON	*Exasperated.* And that is all the thanks I get — after the time and energy I have expended on your behalf. Not to mention a fee owing to the Curator of Miracles. — And what am I supposed to tell the procession of sacred cows and the little girls with garlands? And what will you do? Your position is more than perilous.

> *Pantites stands deep in thought. An idea is taking shape. Geron watches him with interest. Pantites comes suddenly to life again — master of the situation, and, for once, enjoying it.*

PANTITES	Geron, — call them in, Cleon and the others. No — *He pauses, listening to the sounds from the square —* Let us be sure first of our following. *He goes up to the window and looks out cautiously, taking care not to be seen.* I can see the procession, waiting in a side street. And there is a splendid crowd gathering. *He turns to Geron.* Do you think I should make a state appearance — to secure their allegiance, before Cleon thinks of it?

GERON   *Rubbing his hands in delight.* You are learning, boy
                   — you are learning.

                              *Pantites grins at him and steps up to the
                              window.*

GERON   You need not address them — a wave of your hand is all
                   they expect.

PANTITES   Go and summon the Elders — let us have everyone here.

                              *Pantites steps out into full view of the crowd.
                              A storm of cheering greets his appearance.
                              Pantites waves a dignified hand in response.*

                              *Geron beams on him with pride — then he
                              pulls himself sharply together.*

GERON   In a moment I shall become a sentimental loyalist
                   myself!

                              *Geron takes his exit R. Pantites waves again
                              to the crowd. He is beginning to enjoy their
                              acclamation. He turns away from the window
                              — and he is smiling in obvious gratification.
                              Suddenly he realises what is happening to
                              him, and his smile is replaced by shocked
                              dismay.*

PANTITES   Dear heaven — how quickly one comes to enjoy it . . . !

                              *Having realised, he can now laugh a little at
                              the danger past — but the glance he turns
                              towards the window is wary. The cheering
                              from the crowd rings louder, trying to call him
                              back. Cleon enters, followed by Iolaus and
                              Geron. Scorpias and Cleisthenes, whispering
                              between themselves, bring up the rear. Cleon,
                              his face expressionless, gives an involuntary
                              glance towards the window as he hears the
                              acclaim of the crowd, Pantites notes his
                              reaction.*

CLEON   *Courteous in his irony.* We are summoned to audience,
                   I believe?

Pantites looks at him, but makes no reply.
He too, is master now of all the tricks. He
moves casually to pass the window, lingering
a moment to give the crowd a sight of himself.
The cheers rise to a frenzy. After a moment
he turns.

PANTITES   Yes, Cleon. I have been given power absolute . . . and
I wish you to know why I am rejecting it.

SCORPIAS   *Incredulous.* You are — rejecting it . . . ?

PANTITES   *Softly in his surprise, and a little sad.* Yes.

         The others are silent. Iolaus turns away,
         relaxing, with a deep sigh of relief.

CLEON   Your decision, Pantites, shows remarkable sense. And
what now is your intention?

PANTITES   *Carefully, with thought.* To survive, Cleon. To depart
freely from this city — whither, or with what aim, is of
no consequence.

         There is a pause. Cleon gives him a rapid,
         thoughtful glance, then moves down L.C.

CLEON   Pantites, let us not be hasty. Old men one day will need
successors in government . . . You have the wisdom —
and the skill; if you could be persuaded to conform . . .

PANTITES   Who can conform to what is formless? You have nothing
in this city that is real; no truth that does not split itself
in paradox.

IOLAUS   Pantites . . . Truth is a young man's toy; like the sun
through a burning glass, he turns it upon the autumn
waste that once was hope in other men; himself intent,
he disregards the inconstancy of the sun. Truth is an old
man's decoy; like the low red winter sky beyond the
colonnade of the forest, he stumbles after it — knowing
himself beholden to the failing light. Between your age
and ours, we cannot argue what is truth.

         Pantites' eyes travel slowly from his father to
         Geron.

GERON	*Mildly.* I think myself, there is something to be said for achieving a half-good where the best is not allowed.
PANTITES	Geron . . . can the illusion be restored?
GERON	*Very quietly, and grave.* There is a way.
PANTITES	Can it be made to justify my comrades' death?
GERON	Well, it will justify their fame as heroes. You restore the illusion that every man at Thermopylae had his choice, and the others chose to die.
PANTITES	So be it. *He turns.* Cleon, the guilt for their death lies not on you; nor the onus on you, Father, to defend my innocence. Scorpias, bear you the tidings through the city, inventing as you choose the details of the story. Let it be known — Pantites has confessed to cowardice.

There is a reaction from them all at this.

Pantites turns back to the window. Obliterate my name from their memorial, and leave blank the space to commemorate my shame. Build tall the column, that it may be seen from every street; build tall the column, and honour your heroes . . . But let not any living one of you boast of 'the glory of Sparta' the glory is theirs at Thermopylae — leave the wind to sing of it there.

He moves towards the exit L.

End of scene.

A place at the meeting of four roads.

Early morning, some months later.

Behind the bushes, Philander's circus has made its camp. The tops of two gaily coloured tents can be seen, and a plume of smoke from a camp-fire. The circus is breaking camp. Mingling with the morning song of birds is the sound of harness bells, the clanking of pots and pans, voices and laughter. — And somewhere, someone is playing upon the pipes an air from Macedonia. The sun is newly rising, and the sky is coming blue and clear.

Pantites and Geron enter R. pursued by an unseen horde of jeering children.

CHILD
Off. Coward! Rotten old coward!

A shower of stones fall beside them. Geron shakes his fist towards the children.

GERON
Go on — be off with you — embryo monsters! Go on — shelter behind your mothers' skirts — and pray heaven forgive the men who spawned you!

A chorus of shrieks, jeers and hoots of laughter.

PANTITES
Ignore them, and they will tire of the game.

GERON
You are not accommodating a rotten egg down your neck.

In disgust, he gropes inside the hood of his garment.

The squabbling voices of the children, with a few last cries of "coward" fade on the wind.

GERON
How can anyone love children? They have neither morals, wit nor understanding; no sense of justice, of self restraint nor of mercy. They are tormentors, liars and cowards. An untrained pup has nobler instincts.

PANTITES   And they grow to be men. As children, they have at
             least the excuse of knowing no better.

GERON   In every village, the same; stoned by children, set upon
             by the dogs — no bed for us, even in a stable, lest we
             spread moral contagion to the beasts. When did we last
             have a day's work that was not shifting garbage or
             emptying cesspits? Are you not convinced yet that death
             would be preferable?

PANTITES   Preferable. But I made a vow to live, self-confessed to
             cowardice. If this is the way that cowards are used, I am
             in no position to complain.

GERON   Pantites, who now remembers why you took upon
             yourself this living martyrdom? Sparta pursues her
             accustomed ways, forgetful of your brief intrusion. Upon
             the road, who casts their stones with any thought for
             what you symbolize? No-one! You are simply a
             licensed target, to absorb the energy of any local spite
             that happens to be flourishing! Why endure it to so little
             purpose, when the remedy lies in a quick thrust of your
             sword . . .?

PANTITES   *Shakes his head.* I seem to have taken the guilt of the
             world on my shoulders, and I cannot lay it down.

GERON   *Angry in his compassion.* You are not a god! Man, go
             back to Thermopylae and die — before it breaks the
             heart of you.

                    Pantites shakes his head. Geron sighs, rising.

             It is a long road to the world's end.

PANTITES   I have eternity at my disposal.

GERON   The meeting of the four roads . . . take your choice.
             Myself, I like the one that looks towards the hills.

PANTITES   *Rising.* Or the cooler road that dips away between the
             cypresses.

GERON   The road to the hills grows watercresses in its ditch . . .

                    *Philander appears between the bushes, emptying
                    a pail of water.*

PHILANDER	A good morning to you, sirs.
PANTITES	Good morning.
PHILANDER	You are early on the road. Polixenes! Bring a skin of wine — we have company.
PANTITES	Philander!
PHILANDER	Ay, sir — I am Philander . . .
PANTITES	Do you not remember? A thousand years behind us — an inn nearby Thermopylae — ?
PHILANDER	*Delighted.* I remember! Well I remember! You and your friend — the professional philanthropist! *He shakes his hands with enthusiasm.*
GERON	Friend, I have long since been forced out of business. By accident, I became an honest man — and now I find too little charity around me to make philanthropy a paying proposition.
PHILANDER	*Concerned.* Sir — let us not cease to believe in charity, even if we must look back into ourselves to find it. Polixenes! *To Pantites.* Where do you make for this time?
PANTITES	The world's end.

PHILANDER	*Delighted.* Now I do recognise you as a fellow traveller! We all head the same way, but I prefer those who acknowledge it.
	
	    They arrange themselves to sit. Philander is laughing in his pleasure to see them again.
	
	Did I not say our paths would cross again? Once you have met Philander — everywhere you meet Philander. Like the dust in your mouth, you find me on every road — somewhere. Polixenes! — the wine!
	
	    Polixenes scampers into their midst, with the wineskin. He cackles his happy, imbecile

101

laughter as he passes round the wineskin.

GERON   How did you fair at Olympia?

PHILANDER   *Gloomy.* Ah . . . a sorry choice that proved to be! We were delayed upon the way — a dismal tale which I will spare you. The games were over when we reached Olympia — and we lost ahead of us the crowds returning home. I have not, in all my years on the road, known a tour so bedevilled with disaster. It was as if · luck took flight, the day battle was done at Thermopylae . . .

GERON   *A sigh.* I can promise you, it did not come to roost with us!

The dwarf has been trying to attract Philander's attention.

PHILANDER   *Seeing him.* Polixenes — old friends, do you remember? *Polixenes grins at them all — then nudges Philander.* Ay, Polixenes, tell me . . .

The dwarf carefully spells out his message in signs. He whinneys like a horse, indicates the silhouette of pregnancy; points to the sun; draws an arc in the sky; then he ticks off three fingers. Without any difficulty, Philander translates each of these signs into a word.

PHILANDER   The horse — the mare in foal! — days — three. Three days! *He is very pleased with this.* Friends, that luck of ours may be a homing pigeon after all! There is a fair-sized town beyond the ridge — enough for three days business, while the mare drops her foal and the creature finds its marching legs.

To Polixenes.

Convey our thanks to our equine lady, for her consideration.

He translates into signs for the dwarf. He points to himself; clasps his hands; bows; points to the camp, and whinneys like horse. Screeching with delight, the dwarf runs off to deliver his message. Philander calls after him

— And next time, guard our mares more carefully in a stranger's field! *He does not attempt to translate this into sign language, and Polixenes nods and smiles, grasping the gist of it perhaps, if not the message.* Polixenes has never learned the art of speech, but he can translate my meaning to the horses and theirs to me, as if our language were the same. And in his native village they would have burned him as a sorcerer . . . !

PANTITES   *Suddenly.* Philander — what is your direction?

PHILANDER   Homeward — to Macedonia. Not that we have any there who wait for us, but it is a custom we keep, to spend two months of winter in a certain place . . . *He laughs, and confesses it.* — Well, it is a hollow in the hillside we have ringed with stones. It is a foolish thought, but it amuses us — to knot a loop in our road, and call it home.

PANTITES   *Earnestly leaning forward.* Philander — if I told you that my friend and I are seeking work . . .

PHILANDER   *At once, delighted, he springs to his feet.* Friend — Hermes sent you in answer to my prayer! We have for a month been needing to replace two men we had to leave in the care of an innkeeper — they were injured when their wagon was swept away fording the river. In a company as small as ours, every man has a dozen trades — from shoeing horses to stage-managing Apollo's chariot; one man is sorely missed, the loss of two is a catastrophe. *He clasps Pantites on the shoulder.* You need seek no further. Come — I will introduce you to the company.

PANTITES   *Swiftly.* Sir — one moment — *He rises.*

PHILANDER   You have no skill? What of it? You will learn, a talent for hard work is all you need — and good humour. Most of all, good humour. And for your friend — *he laughs* — Oh, I can tell you now the job I have for you — !

PANTITES   Philander! I must ask — do you know of me? My name and reputation?

PHILANDER   Did you not tell me that you were a Spartan? . . . I think I did hear a while ago the echo of some tale. *He scratches his head, trying to remember. Pantites watches him,*

103

tense. Geron goes to Pantites urgently.

GERON   Take for once your chance — it may not come again.

PANTITES   *Very still, watching Philander.* My name, sir, is —
               Pantites.

PHILANDER   *All is remembered.* Ay — that was the name. And you
               told me yourself, that you were at Thermopylae.
               Myself, I do not pay much attention to gossip that
               swirls along the road — like dust, whipped up,
               dispersed, and left to make new patterns.

PANTITES   Sir . . . what is your answer?

PHILANDER   Coward — hero — pah! Just words! Will you take more
               than your share of food — or hide when work is
               waiting? Will you torment Polixenes? — drive too hard
               the horses? — or do any of those things that make a
               man less of a man? No! I am sure of it! Then you are
               the man for me. *He turns into the gap between the
               bushes.*

PANTITES   *Joyful, almost to the point of tears.* Geron! Can you
               believe it? We are homeward bound — with friends —
               for Macedonia . . .

PHILANDER   *Stopping suddenly in the gap.* Wait! Before you meet
               the company, we must find for you a name . . .

                    Chilled, Pantites stops.

PANTITES   I have a name.

PHILANDER   *Drily.* Ay, indeed you have! Oh, it is no matter. I will
               introduce as Pantites — the company will find a nick-
               name for you soon enough. No-one in the Circus is
               allowed to keep for long the name his parents gave him!
               *Smiling, he urges Pantites towards the gap — then he sees
               Pantites face. Philander is dismayed.* Friend! What have I
               said to cause you so much pain? If you identity is of so
               little consequence to me, can it matter so much more
               to you?

PANTITES   It matters.

PHILANDER	*Soberly.* Ay — it matters. Let it be known we have Pantites in our midst, and in a month I shall be out of business. A word — like coward or hero — it matters, yet it matters not, and here we waste good breath upon it! Pantites . . . no, I cannot say I like it greatly as a name . . . Come, let us find you a better.
GERON	Pantites, for the love of heaven, accept this man's condition.
PANTITES	I cannot.
GERON	You insist upon life — yet will not accept that one small compromise that could make life endurable!
PANTITES	*Distracted.* I cannot, like a garment, lay aside myself and put on a new identity.
GERON	Why not? Who is there now to care, if your name be left to blow like a discarded leaf along the road?
PANTITES	*Very quietly.* My comrades.
GERON	Your comrades are dead; however loud your solitary clash of arm, it will not sound across the Styx to waken them.
PANTITES	I am the last of the three hundred. My name is the last shout of defiance from the Spartan line; This square of ground — here, between my feet! — this is Thermopylae. I hold it till I die.
	There is a pause. Philander frowns in thought.
PHILANDER	If I had no-one to consider but myself . . .
	Polixenes enters with another wineskin and a large hunk of coarse bread. He pauses questioningly beside Philander, who puts an arm about his shoulders.
	The circus is their livelihood, you see . . .
PANTITES	You have nothing for me?
PHILANDER	I have nothing for you Pantites of Sparta.

> *A silence. Polixenes tries to offer the bread to Pantites. Pantites, half conscious of him, finds himself taking it. Philander glances up thoughtfully.*

PHILANDER   Unless . . . *He considers, then shakes his head.*

PANTITES   Unless?

PHILANDER   No — the suggestion would offend you.

PANTITES   I am past offence.

PHILANDER   *Reluctantly.* It is only a question of foiling public prejudice, you see . . . I am a showman, and I know. By giving it the name of entertainment, you can sell what would start a war if offered seriously. Now, beside Polixenes here, we have the Bearded Lady; the Twins, lovely girls, but joined together at the waist; and the Hairy Man. A small group, all — like yourself — dispossessed of the world. With them I could find a place for you. Oh, nothing vulgar, you understand — just a small booth, with a sign, "The Man from Thermopylae". The public will love it. They will want to hear about the battle while their children give you apples — those same people who would stone you in the street outside.

PANTITES   *With infinite pain.* I see. I thank you for your kindness, Philander.

> *Polixenes, with a screech of laughter, swings on Philander's hands. Philander does not take his eyes from Pantites.*

PHILANDER   I have offended you.

PANTITES   I am not offended.

PHILANDER   In my company we have no freak show. All are artist's, making use of whatever talent or attribute nature gave them. A dwarf in his small stature has a gift from chance as rare as that of any man who happens to be born a king.

GERON	Yet for all the truth in that, I think it troubles you.
PHILANDER	*A sigh — then frankly.* Ay, sir, it does. It is the basest instinct in humanity that gapes at the grotesque — and here we are, trading upon it. Often I am tempted to disband the troop, but then — the circus is their only refuge. Always they plead to stay, asking what will become of them if I forsake them, too. So there you have it, sir, and where the right of it lies, I know not.
GERON	The blessing of the gods be upon you, sir.
PHILANDER	Your friend seems ill —
PANTITES	No — I thank you — I am well. I must be on my way. *He is anxious now to be gone.*
	Philander looks at him uneasily, but there is nothing he can say or do. Philander glances behind him.
PHILANDER	Those tents are not down yet, I see. I had planned to be well upon the road by noon. *He takes Polixenes by the hand. Geron offers the wineskin to him, but Philander waves it aside.* Nay, friend — take it. You will have need of it upon the way — I know those roads. Good day to you. And may the gods go with you.
GERON	The blessing of Hermes upon you, sir.
	Philander gives one last glance at Pantites, but Pantites is sunk in some desolate world of his own. Philander disappears with Polixenes behind the bushes. There comes the sound of the voice briskly giving orders round the camp. One of the tents sways and disappears. By the end of the scene, the second tent, too, is gone.
GERON	Take heart, Pantites. You have not met such kindness since you left Thermopylae.
PANTITES	No . . . and if that man's charity can find no place for me, where is it to be found in all the world?

GERON   *Taking his arm with the gentle firmness of inevitability.*
This is the road back to Thermopylae . . .

> *Geron leads Pantites off, Pantites' feet
> dragging. The dwarf and the bearded lady
> appear behind the bushes and wave sadly
> after them as they depart into the distance.*

> *End of scene.*

SCENE 3

A desolate place upon the cliffs above Thermopylae.

Evening, some days later.

Even the red light of the dying sun can bring no warmth to such a place. The rocks are harsh in outline, their shadows black. The only sound is of the moaning wind, the wailing seabirds and the wash of the sea below.

Geron and Pantites enter, Pantites limping a little from the old wound in his leg. His manner, though weary, is one of relief — almost cheerfulness. He goes to the edge of the cliff up C. and looks down. He is quiet a moment.

PANTITES Who could have the thought that I should be so glad to see again this place? *He points out to Geron familiar landmarks on the shore below.* See, Geron — there is a Phocian Wall where we held the Persians. And there — just below us, do you see? — the hillock where we made our last stand. *He pauses, remembering — then he laughs a little.* For all that it was the end of the world for us, we were a cheerful company that morning. A scout came in, reporting the enemy so numerous that a shower of his arrows would hide the sun. And Dionekes leaped up, roaring — 'Good! We shall fight 'em in the shade!' *He laughs.* Poor old Dionekes! If he had an ambition, it was to be remembered as a wit . . . and now he is become a hero, no one will ever dare to laugh at his jokes again.

A pause.

Well, I have kept them waiting long enough. *He draws his sword.*

GERON You are determined.

PANTITES As you said, Geron, I am not a god. I am only a man — and sick to the heart of being alone.

GERON Well, I came only to observe — not to pass opinion.

109

PANTITES   Are you disappointed?

GERON   Why should I be? I foresaw this for your end.

PANTITES   I must be on my way. *He looks down at the shore.*
                There they lie, my friends . . . and who could
                distinguish now, Greek bones from Persian? And they,
                Geron? — I wonder, do they care at all? Do they still
                mount guard upon their separate camps — or do they
                mingle and gossip together in Elysium? Who knows,
                perhaps they will hold a reunion dinner for me tonight
                . . . ! *He is gay and happy at the thought, impatient
                now to be gone. He is about to start his scramble down
                to the shore, when he is arrested by a voice from the
                distance.*

OLD WOMAN   *Off. Shouting.* You there — stranger! One moment —

PANTITES   What is it? I am in haste.

                        *The old woman enters L. carrying a swathed
                        bundle. She is breathless after her climb.*

OLD WOMAN   Are you descending to the shore?

PANTITES   Yes. What do you want?

OLD WOMAN   Why — I know your face — ! You are the soldier —

PANTITES   And you the innkeeper on the road to Sparta — I
                remember.

                        *The baby's cry sounds from the bundle in
                        her arms.*

                What have you there?

OLD WOMAN   That child — the serving girl's brat. She pined so for that
                man of hers, she lost her wits completely. Threw herself
                from these very cliffs a week ago.

PANTITES   Apollo have mercy upon her.

OLD WOMAN   Ach, she will get no prayers from me —selfish bitch!
                Look what she left on my hands! As if I have not had
                enough . . . I reared four of my own an packed 'em off

into the world, and not one penny's worth of help did I get from any of their fathers. I have not patience to start rearing brats again. As you are going down to the shore, take the child with you and save my legs a journey. Lay it somewhere the tide will not reach it — and below a rock, to give it shade. Let the poor thing die in comfort.

She holds out the bundle to Pantites.

PANTITES   And you will abandon it to the mercy of the wind and the long night?

GERON   It is an old and honoured custom.

PANTITES   What offence has the child committed?

OLD WOMAN   It should never have got itself born in the first place. But it is the war — this always happens in a war. Let it die and cancel out the error. I must get back. There is all the baking to be done for tomorrow's wedding party . . .

She departs the way she has come. Pantites stands very still, looking down at the baby.

GERON   You have your instructions.

PANTITES   Always it is the war! Or the government. Or the oracle. Or the army. Or the school we attended . . . It is never ourselves.

GERON   And why do you think we have a social system, if it is not to save ourselves the effort of thinking?

PANTITES   Society! I am talking about you — and me — and that old woman —

GERON   — And your father and your uncle and your sister!

PANTITES   My father gave me something . . . as Sparta gave me something — I suppose . . . I had twenty-five tolerable years before they condemned me to death. But this ill-fortuned little wretch — *He stoops to pick up the baby.*

111

GERON   Is it not your responsibility.

                   Moving to a flat rock up C. on the edge of
                   the cliff, Geron mounts it, casting a downward
                   glance to the shore.

PANTITES   *Driving his sword into the·sheath to free his arms for*
                   the child. It is my responsibility! As the bones on the
                   battlefield are my responsibility.

GERON   You cannot answer for the sins of the world.

PANTITES   I am . . . the sin of the world.

                   He is upon one knee beside the baby. Now he
                   adjusts its wrappings, making it comfortable.
                   He has his back to Geron, and his head down.
                   Then he hears the wind. He raises his head
                   sharply looking upward and away from Geron.

                   Puzzled and a little uneasy. Geron, listen — do you hear
                   the wind?

                   The wind starts as a whisper, rising to hurricane
                   volume in a matter of seconds — suggestive
                   of something that has come from infinite
                   distance at incredible speed, an immense
                   noise, filling both stage and auditorium. It
                   causes no movement, and cannot be felt.
                   Baffled, Pantites looks this way and that,
                   seeking indication of the wind's direction. His
                   attention distracted by this eerie phenomenon,
                   he does not notice the action of Geron behind
                   him. Geron, quite casually as any other actor
                   would, removes his beard and wig. Then he
                   peels off his ragged mantle, to reveal a simple,
                   shining white tunic — irridescent or luminous
                   — and the feathered white wings at the heels
                   of his sandals. He has none of the other
                   traditional accessories. The old man's stoop
                   vanishes, leaving him with the physique of an
                   athletic man. During this operation, floodlights
                   concealed in the rocks about his feet and
                   above his head, concentrate upon the figure
                   to full power. When the leisurely transformation
                   is complete, the light should be at full — and
                   the sound of the wind at hurricane pitch is
                   suddenly faded out. It is Hermes, messenger of
                   the Gods, radiant as the morning and

112

                    completely unperturbed, as he stands with
                    Geron's costume over his arm, waiting for
                    Pantites to turn and recognise him.

                    The sudden silence and the radiance from
                    behind him, tell Pantites all he needs to
                    know. Very still now, he is afraid to turn
                    and raise his eyes. Hermes, to encourage him,
                    delicately drops the Geron costume on to
                    the floor beside Pantites. Pantites, still on
                    his knees, turns slowly without looking up
                    — and so it is upon the winged sandals that
                    his eye falls. Incredulous, he puts out a hand
                    to touch them — drawing it back quickly
                    before making contact.

PANTITES   *Remembering.* Winged sandals . . . white, like goose feathers . . . *He looks up at Hermes, but the light dazzles him. He has to look away, shading his eyes — and then his glance falls on the rags, wig and beard that Geron wore. He picks them up slowly, tenderly, and with sadness.* And did my friend have no more reality than this . . . ?

HERMES   *Moved.* Did I play the part too well? Forgive me.

PANTITES   *Making the best of it.* I suppose it is not every day that one shares breakfast with a god . . . But I valued Geron more for thinking him a man.

                    Gently he lets the costume fall from his hand.

HERMES   *Quietly.* I know. One comes so easily to love what is imperfect; that I have discovered. It is something which my father Zeus, who is more remote from men, can never understand.

                    They look at each other, and this time Pantites
                    is not blinded by the radiance.
                    There is a pause. Then he rises.

PANTITES   *Looking at the baby on the ground as he speaks.* Why did you preserve me on the battlefield?

HERMES   Once, long ago, it was a vow I made, to appease the wrath of my father Zeus against the human race, that

	I would find one honest man. I have to do it periodically.
PANTITES	*Without reproach, but rather tired.* And do you always put him to the test so thoroughly?
HERMES	How else do you prove a species worth preserving?
PANTITES	*Weary, he shakes his head, expelling the words on a sigh.* I have no idea.
HERMES	*Much the same tone.* Looking down upon the battlefield, I saw a helmet flash for a moment in the sun. How was I to know the man beneath the helmet would be you?
PANTITES	Hermes, you would be saying that to any man whose life you had shared for a twelvemonth.
HERMES	Does that make it any easier? *A pause.* However, if it is any consolation to you, you — and I — have bought the earth's survival for another week — a day — a millenium . . . *A sigh.* I hope you think your fellow men are worth it.
PANTITES	*A shrug.* I answer only for myself. But there is the baby, I cannot leave him. *He drops to his knee to pick it up. He gives a slight, sidelong smile at Hermes.* And you never know, he might turn out better.
HERMES	He rarely does.
PANTITES	But he might. In thirty years' time, come back and see. *He gathers up the baby and rises to his feet.*
HERMES	What message do I carry to the dead?
PANTITES	My comrades? Ask them . . . ask them to postpone that reunion supper. I have other duties. *Holding the baby, he stares down the road ahead of him. His eyes are bleak.*

HERMES	*Watching him.* You are sure you do not want to change your mind? Apollo will take the baby — he will feel no pain.
	Pantites, standing with his back to Hermes, shakes his head.
	I would lay a banquet for you — tonight upon Olympus . . .
	Again Pantites shakes his head.
	I offered Zeus the suffering of one man; but if I asked him, he would let me trade the world and buy you back.
PANTITES	*Still with his back to Hermes.* Hermes . . . I am not equipped to deal with Cosmic complications. There is a baby here which must be somehow washed and fed and bedded for the night. It must be reared and taught and housed, until it is of age. It must be loved, too, I suppose . . . *He looks at it, baffled a moment — then shrugs.* If there is no-one else to do these things, then obviously I must. What construction you and your father, Zeus, put upon the situation, is entirely up to you. *He adjusts the bundle more comfortably in his arm.* It grows dark. I must find a shelter for the child. *He turns looking at Hermes.* You . . . do not come my way . . . ?
HERMES	*Shaking his head.* No, Pantites, you go alone.
	Aware now of the impending loss, Pantites looks from Hermes to the fallen rags of Geron on the ground. Hermes' eyes follow his.
	That is all you will remember; dimly; an old, drunken beggar, to whom you showed a kindness on the road. Even as you turn away, my face is slipping from your memory — *Suddenly.* — Pantites — wait!
	Pantites turns.
	One promise I will make — for friendship's sake, and the laughter shared upon the road. *He makes the slightest gesture of his hand, drawing Pantites towards him.* Give me your youth — *He touches him lightly upon the cheeks —* and your cloak to wrap it in.
	Pantites takes off his cloak and hands it to him.
	There — so I shall hoard it for you; and when you are tired and crammed with years, I will not let them send the grey old ferryman to summon you. I will come

myself in the shape you knew me, and we will set out together upon the road as in some morning from a memory.

There is one long parting glance between them, then slowly Pantites turns his back upon Hermes. Even as he turns, he forgets the figure on the rock, and he is just a man in a tattered soldier's uniform, bearing, incongruously, a baby in his arms.

The light around Hermes dims and blacks out, and his last words are spoken from the darkness.

The last red gleam from the evening sun falls upon Pantites, alone, and departing back the way he came through the auditorium.

The voice of Hermes follows him.

HERMES   Go your way, man, as I first saw you — wearing honesty like a garland. And if that garland prick your brow, bear it as best you may . . . for you are the hope of the world.

The end.